LOVE

A Collection of Poetry and Prose
on Loving and Being in Love

Compiled by Robin Barratt

With...

Akwu Sunday Victor, Alan Murphy, Alasdair S. Goudie, Angharad Thompson Rees, Andrew Hunter, Barbara Hawthorn, Bee Parkinson, Bernadette Perez, Brian Langley, Brigette Furlonger, Carol Ann, Cath Bore, Catherine Morgans, Chris Kempling, Clare Lightfoot, Clement Clark, Courtney Speedy, Darren Sharp, David Hollywood, David Watt, Dayle Ashton, Dominique Megane Clinckemaille, Don Adams, Ella Edwards, Elspeth Glenday, Farha A. Jaleel, Frank Cardiff, Frank Meintjies, Greg Bogaerts, Guy Morris, Heidi Al Khajah, Helen Bowers, Hunter Armstrong, Jacky Perez, James Scalise, Jenna Rainey, Jennifer Riggs, Jessica L. Jackson, Joe Gallagher, John Karl Stokes, John R. Sabine, John Stockdill, Jo Wilson-Ridley, Justin Fox, Karin Slater, Karishma Krishna Kumar, Kariuki wa Nyamu, Kathleen Bleakley, Kathleen Boyle, Kathleen Coyle, Kathleen Vallance, Katie Lewington, Keith Nunes, Kev Milsom, Kimmy Alan, Kirsty A. Niven, Leon Stelmach, Lonita Nugrahayu, Lucy Reid, Madhumitha Murali, Mandy Mullen, Marc Brightside, Martin Redfern, Maxine Rose Munro, Megan Costigan, Megan MacLeod, Michelle Lee, Molly Donald, Nikita Krishna Kumar, Nilanjana Bose, Norbert Gora, Pab Roberts, Pallang Mofokeng, Pamela Scott, Rachel Walker, Rhyl Graham, Ronald L Kundinger, Rosie Mapplebeck, Ryan Joel, S'busiso Manqa, Sara Spivey, Steve Howrie, Trudy Duffy – Wigman, Vaijayantee Bhattacharya, Zahra Zuhair and Zondrae King.

Published by Robin Barratt
© Robin Barratt 2016 and all the authors herein

All rights reserved. No part of this publication may be reproduced,
distributed, or transmitted in any form or by any means,
including photocopying, recording, or other electronic or mechanical methods,
without the prior written permission of the publisher,
except in the case of brief quotations embodied in critical reviews and
certain other non-commercial uses permitted by copyright law.
For permission requests, email the publisher at the address below.

W: www.collectionsofpoetryandprose.com
E: Editor@collectionsofpoetryandprose.com
E: RobinBarratt@yahoo.com

Committed to publishing the works and words of writers and poets around the world

Special Thanks To...

The Bahrain Writers' Circle (BahrainWritersCircle.com); The Second Circle; Huntly Writers, Aberdeenshire, Scotland (Huntlywriters.co.uk); Donny O'Rourke's Barrington Bards poetry group in Glasgow, Scotland; Lismore Poetry Group, Republic of Ireland; Alberta Romance Writers' Association, Calgary, Canada, (Albertaromancewriters.com); Australian Bush Poet's Association (ABPA.org.au); The Gold Coast Writers Association (Goldcoastwriters.org); PEN South Africa (Pensouthafrica.co.za); the Kinwriters; the Centre for Contemporary Arts, Glasgow (cca-glasgow.com); International Writers' Workshop, New Zealand (Iww.co.nz); Scottish Poetry Library (Scottishpoetrylibrary.org.uk); South African Writers College (Sawriterscollege.co.za); Interior Authors Group, British Columbia, Canada (Interiorauthorsgroup.wordpress.com); Scottish Book Trust (Scottishbooktrust.com); London Writers' Cafe; Trish Hopkinson; Suzanne Anderson; New Zealand Writers' College (Nzwriterscollege.co.nz); Poets House, New York, USA (PoetsHouse.org); Jeffrey Thorpe at the Centenary Writer Group; ACT Writers Society, Braddon, Australia (actwriters.org.au); Writers online (Writers-online.co.uk); Australian Capital Territory Writers Centre (Actwriters.org.au); *Writing* Magazine... some of whose poets and writers contributed to this book after notices were kindly sent out to their members. Thank you!

Contents By Title...

Introduction by Robin Barratt. Page 12

When I First Saw You by *Anonymous*. Page 15
Today by Rachel Walker. Page 16
Love by Andrew Hunter. Page 18
Fifty Years by Brian Langley. Page 19
Love by Dayle Ashton. Page 21
Break Out by Greg Bogaerts. Page 22
Empty Rooms by Maxine Rose Munro. Page 24
Love Haiku by Kimmy Alan. Page 25
Wedding by Kirsty A. Niven. Page 26
Is This Love? by Pamela Scott. Page 27
The Temple by Pab Roberts. Page 33
Love's Transmission by David Watt. Page 35
My Darling Love by Jessica L. Jackson. Page 36
Love by Kathleen Vallance. Page 37
Awakening by Ryan Joel. Page 38
Chagall's Village by Alan Murphy. Page 39
The Perfect Couple by Katie Lewington. Page 40
Tell Me It's Real by Molly Donald. Page 41
Love by Vaijayantee Bhattacharya. Page 43
Hanging On by Kathleen Boyle. Page 44
Your Arms Are The Walls by Courtney Speedy. Page 47
The Book by Lonita Nugrahayu. Page 48
Synonym by Nilanjana Bose. Page 49
Time Heals All by John R. Sabine. Page 50
Live And Love by Steve Howrie. Page 51
If I Could by S'busiso Manqa. Page 52
Black Cream For Ruined Hearts by David Hollywood. Page 54
Meeting On The Footpath by Keith Nunes. Page 55
Llandudno Pier by Andrew Hunter. Page 56
Kasia By The Seashore by Marc Brightside. Page 57
Be It Your Love Is Gold by Pallang Mofokeng. Page 58
One Word Only by Sara Spivey. Page 59
My Love by Akwu Sunday Victor. Page 61
Midnight Stroll By The Canal by Pamela Scott. Page 63
Organising Functions And Principles Of Love by Ian McKenzie. Page 64
The Breakup by Ronald L Kundinger. Page 65
The Love For My Niece by Heidi Al Khajah. Page 66
The Extraordinary Love Poem by Kariuki wa Nyamu. Page 67
Love. Full Stop by Mandy Mullen. Page 69

A Love That's True by Frank Cardiff. Page 71
Compare You To A Rose by David Watt. Page 72
He Is by Kirsty A. Niven. Page 73
A Little Tin by John Stockdill. Page 74
The Colour Of Love by Clement Clark. Page 75
Lasting Love by Jennifer Riggs. Page 76
Alison's Whispers by Keith Nunes. Page 77
Weary-eyed Wanderers by Jenna Rainey. Page 78
Broken Promises by Farha A. Jaleel. Page 79
Bound By Thread by Jacky Perez. Page 81
Chat by Brigette Furlonger. Page 84
Love Is A Dream by Dominique Megane Clinckemaille. Page 85
The Birth Of Signs by Alan Murphy. Page 86
Fire And Desire by Chris Kempling. Page 87
Hello, I'm In Eastleigh by Marc Brightside. Page 88
Wild And Innocent by Dayle Ashton. Page 89
Come Love Me Between The Sheets by Courtney Speedy. Page 90
The Artist by Angharad Thompson Rees. Page 92
On The Bridge As Darkness Falls by Clare Lightfoot. Page 93
Midnight by Katie Lewington. Page 96
Home by Kirsty A. Niven. Page 97
Forgiveness by Elspeth Glenday. Page 98
All The World's A War-Zone by Nilanjana Bose. Page 99
Let Go by S'busiso Manqa. Page 100
Open Window by Bernadette Perez. Page 101
Evanescent by Lonita Nugrahayu. Page 102
Here Comes The Bride by Barbara Hawthorn. Page 103
Sparkage by Pamela Scott. Page 105
No Greater Love by Rhyl Graham. Page 106
Petals Linger by Kathleen Boyle. Page 108
The Memory Of Desire by Ronald L Kundinger. Page 109
Untitled by Leon Stelmach. Page 110
Murmuration by Alan Murphy. Page 111
Never Together Forever by Kimmy Alan. Page 112
My Father's Call by Justin Fox. Page 113
She by Ryan Joel. Page 114
Fall For Me by Courtney Speedy. Page 115
2 Lovers Now Entwined by Megan MacLeod. Page 116
Good Morning by Carol Ann. Page 117
Solstice by Jenna Rainey. Page 118
Muse by Joe Gallagher. Page 119
Love's Young Dream by Frank Cardiff. Page 120
Storms Of The Heart by Bee Parkinson Page 121
Cruelty by Lonita Nugrahayu. Page 123
Love Keeps No Record Of Wrongs by Lucy Reid. Page 124

Evanescence by Andrew Hunter. Page 125
Love by Madhumitha Murali. Page 126
Midnight Thoughts by Heidi Al Khajah. Page 127
A Friend For All Seasons by Don Adams. Page 128
Season Of The Heart by Frank Meintjies. Page 130
Continue by Katie Lewington. Page 131
Malevolence In Love by David Hollywood. Page 132
The Air by Lonita Nugrahayu. Page 133
My Universe by Angharad Thompson Rees. Page 134
Oswald by Kev Milsom. Page 135
Birds Of My Heart by John R. Sabine. Page 138
Lovely Motivation by S'busiso Manqa. Page 139
The Trouble With Love. By Pamela Scott. Page 140
What If All The Stars Went Out? by Jenna Rainey. Page 141
Warning Shot by Michelle Lee. Page 142
You, My Poetry by Lonita Nugrahayu. Page 144
Luminous by Keith Nunes. Page 145
Mornings by Brian Langley. Page 146
Sorry by Courtney Speedy. Page 147
Naked by Pamela Scott. Page 150
My Love Hive by Kariuki wa Nyamu. Page 151
Bolivia by Kathleen Boyle. Page 152
Ecliptic by Rosie Mapplebeck. Page 153
Love's Malaise by David Watt. Page 154
30th September, 2013 by Kirsty A. Niven. Page 155
The Great Compatibility Quiz by Jennifer Riggs. Page 156
Love's Not A Christmas Thing by Nilanjana Bose. Page 159
Calypso's Lament by Helen Bowers. Page 160
Soul Song by Ryan Joel. Page 161
My Popsicle Toes by Clement Clark. Page 162
Pink Ladies Gossiping by Keith Nunes. Page 163
Love Alive by Dayle Ashton. Page 164
Waiting by Ronald L Kundinger. Page 165
Schnorthog and Schweethog by James Scalise. Page 166
Say It by Guy Morris. Page 167
Met On The Net by Barbara Hawthorn. Page 168
Sustain by Andrew Hunter. Page 170
Beloved by Frank Meintjies. Page 171
Loving You by Akwu Sunday Victor. Page 172
The Day We Sang Love by S'busiso Manqa. Page 173
My Love - For Wine! by David Hollywood. Page 175
I'm Standing At The Cross by Courtney Speedy. Page 176
Time Lapse by Helen Bowers. Page 178
The Moment Of Passion's Fading by Barbara Hawthorn. Page 179
New York Number One by Kathleen Boyle. Page 180

This Thing Inside Me by S'busiso Manqa. Page 181
Newborn by Kirsty A. Niven. Page 182
The Pyramid Of Me by Kimmy Alan. Page 183
The Last Dance by Chris Kempling. Page 184
Change by Katie Lewington. Page 187
Blueberry by Clement Clark. Page 188
A Touch Above by Keith Nunes. Page 189
Those Rad Friends by Molly Donald. Page 190
A Settled Sonnet by Kirsty A. Niven. Page 191
You, Me... Us by S'busiso Manqa. Page 192
The Dancers by Barbara Hawthorn. Page 193
Natalie by Hunter Armstrong. Page 195
You Call To Me As Water by Ronald L Kundinger. Page 199
She Feels Him At A Seaside Motel by John Karl Stokes. Page 200
Puppy Love by Frank Cardiff. Page 201
Love by Frank Meintjies. Page 202
Musings by Katie Lewington. Page 203
My Form Of Loving by Alasdair S. Goudie. Page 204
Desolations Ancient Waste by David Hollywood. Page 206
Tiny Bud by Angharad Thompson Rees. Page 210
Wet And Wild by Dayle Ashton. Page 211
Tender Reeds By The River By Akwu Sunday Victor. Page 212
Pockets Of The Heart by Ella Edwards. Page 214
The Names by Zahra Zuhair. Page 216
Memories Rekindled by David Watt. Page 217
How Could I Fail To See? by Kariuki wa Nyamu. Page 218
Splashdown by Helen Bowers. Page 220
Stolen by Cath Bore. Page 221
Motivation by Rosie Mapplebeck. Page 222
Sushi For Tea by Trudy Duffy - Wigman. Page 223
Tràigh Mhòr by Karin Slater. Page 227
Do You Believe In Soul Mates? by Nikita Krishna Kumar. Page 228
Flair to Share by Catherine Morgans. Page 229
The Tone Of Your Voice by Martin Redfern. Page 230
Baby by Kathleen Coyle. Page 231
To Get Close To You by Dayle Ashton. Page 236
Xanthippe by Pab Roberts. Page 237
Kiss by Kimmy Alan. Page 238
Seven Years Four Days Eleven Months by Rachel Walker. Page 239
Coast Road by Kathleen Bleakley. Page 241
Exotic Love by Jacky Perez. Page 242
Hidden Under The Cloak Of Love by Norbert Gora. Page 243
Plaza Girl by Greg Bogaerts. Page 244
Walter by John Stockdill. Page 246

Hair by Bee Parkinson. Page 247
A Romance by John Karl Stokes. Page 249
The Third Woman by Darren Sharp. Page 250
I Am A Candle by Dayle Ashton. Page 252
A Love Lost by Megan MacLeod. Page 253
Crash by Megan Costigan. Page 254
Roman Love by Jo Wilson-Ridley. Page 255
Sunset by Brian Langley. Page 256
Our Billy by John Stockdill. Page 257
Love On High by David Watt. Page 258
The Going From The Valley by John Karl Stokes. Page 259
From Your Loving Daughter by Karishma Krishna Kumar. Page 260
Til Death Us Do Part by Jenna Rainey. Page 262
Lust-Less Love by Kariuki wa Nyamu. Page 264
Last Goodbye by Angharad Thompson Rees. Page 265
The Last Bye by Nikita Krishna Kumar. Page 266
After Love by Pamela Scott. Page 267
Do You Think Of Me? by Zondrae King. Page 269
Too Broken To Bend by Karishma Krishna Kumar. Page 271
Sometimes by Molly Donald. Page 272
The End by Barbara Hawthorn. Page 273

Contributors' Biographies. Page 274

Contents By Author...

Akwu Sunday Victor. Pages 61, 172, 212
Alan Murphy. Pages 39, 86, 111
Alasdair S. Goudie. Page 204
Andrew Hunter. Pages 18, 56, 125
Angharad Thompson Rees. Pages 92, 134, 210, 265
Barbara Hawthorn. Pages 103, 168, 179, 193, 273
Bee Parkinson. Pages 121, 247
Bernadette Perez. Page 101
Brian Langley. Pages 19, 146, 256
Brigette Furlonger. Page 84
Carol Ann. Page 117
Cath Bore. Page 221
Catherine Morgans. Page 229
Chris Kempling. Page 87, 184
Clare Lightfoot. Page 93
Clement Clark. Pages 75, 162, 188
Courtney Speedy. Pages 47, 90, 115, 147, 176
Darren Sharp. Page 250
David Hollywood. Pages 54, 132, 175, 206
David Watt. Pages 35, 72, 154, 217, 258
Dayle Ashton. Pages 21, 89, 164, 211, 236, 252
Dominique Megane Clinckemaille. Page 85
Don Adams. Page 128
Ella Edwards. Page 214
Elspeth Glenday. Page 98
Farha A. Jaleel. Page 79
Frank Cardiff. Page 71, 120, 201
Frank Meintjies. Pages 130, 171, 202
Greg Bogaerts. Pages 22, 244
Guy Morris. Page 167
Heidi Al Khajah. Pages 66, 127
Helen Bowers. Pages 160, 178, 220
Hunter Armstrong. Page 195
Jacky Perez. Pages 81, 242
James Scalise. Page 166
Jenna Rainey. Pages 78, 118, 141, 262
Jennifer Riggs. Pages 76, 156
Jessica L Jackson. Page 36
Jo Wilson-Ridley. Page 255
Joe Gallagher. Page 119
John Karl Stokes. Pages 200, 249, 259
John R. Sabine. Pages 50, 138

John Stockdill. Pages 74, 246, 257
Jo Wilson-Ridley. Page 255
Justin Fox. Page 113
Karin Slater. Page 227
Karishma Krishna Kumar. Pages 260, 271
Kariuki wa Nyamu. Pages 67, 151, 218, 264
Kathleen Bleakley. Page 241
Kathleen Boyle. Pages 44, 108, 152, 180
Kathleen Coyle. Page 231
Kathleen Vallance. Page 37
Katie Lewington. Pages 40, 96, 131, 187, 203
Keith Nunes. Pages 55, 77, 145, 163, 189
Kev Milsom. Page 135
Kimmy Alan. Pages 25, 112, 183, 238
Kirsty A. Niven. Pages 26, 73, 97, 155, 182, 191
Leon Stelmach. Page 110
Lonita Nugrahayu. Pages 48, 102, 123, 133, 144
Lucy Reid. Page 124
Madhumitha Murali. Page 126
Mandy Mullen. Page 69
Marc Brightside. Page 57, 88
Martin Redfern. Page 230
Maxine Rose Munro. Page 24
Megan Costigan. Page 254
Megan MacLeod. Pages 116, 253
Michelle Lee. Page 142
Molly Donald. Page 41, 190, 272
Nikita Krishna Kumar. Pages 228, 266
Nilanjana Bose. Pages 49, 99, 159
Norbert Gora. Page 243
Pab Roberts. Pages 33, 237
Pallang Mofokeng. Page 58
Pamela Scott. Pages 27, 63, 105, 140, 150, 267
Rachel Walker. Pages 16, 239
Rhyl Graham. Page 106
Ronald L Kundinger. Pages 65, 109, 165, 199
Rosie Mapplebeck. Pages 153, 222
Ryan Joel. Pages 38, 114, 161
S'busiso Manqa. Pages 52, 100, 139, 173, 181, 192
Sara Spivey. Page 59
Steve Howrie. Page 51
Trudy Duffy - Wigman. Page 223
Vaijayantee Bhattacharya. Page 43
Zahra Zuhair. Page 216
Zondrae King. Page 269

Introduction
By Robin Barratt

Welcome to *LOVE - A Collection of Poetry and Prose on Loving and Being in Love*, the second of the **Collections of Poetry and Prose** book series.

Following on from our first collection; *LONELY - A Collection of Poetry and Prose on Loneliness and Being Alone*, *LOVE* is another varied and unique collection of poetry and short prose from writers and poets around the world including: Australia, Bahrain, Canada, Egypt, England, India, Indonesia, Ireland, Italy, Kenya, Netherlands, New Zealand, Pakistan, Poland, Scotland, South Africa, Sri Lanka, Tanzanian, the USA, Wales and a few others. *LOVE* is a wonderful, unique and eclectic mixture of both traditional and modern verse, as well as the more abstract and esoteric, with many of the contributions reflecting the diverse backgrounds and cultures of the contributors; demonstrating that love and loving is certainly not the same for everyone, everywhere in the world!

There are so very many brilliant and brilliantly talented writers out there who never get their works seen or their words read, and so our objectives with this book series is to showcase poets and writers around the world, and to offer them another platform to display their work. It doesn't matter where you live, your age, your culture or your writing experience, we are committed to seeing your work printed and that your words are read.

I am not a poet; I cannot think the way a poet does. I have tried but my mind just doesn't work that way, but I do enjoy reading poetry and in marvelling at how each writer has managed to describe things, feelings and thoughts just by using a few carefully chosen words and well structured sentences. Writing poetry is an extremely individual and personal process, with few (if any) rules and regulations, and so, like in *LONELY*, I have kept almost every poetry contribution exactly as sent, regardless of structure, punctuation and capitalisation. This is the poet's work, and not mine to alter! I have also accepted work from almost every contributor, regardless of the contributors' skill and experience; my ambitions are to see writers' work published and read, and certainly not to judge, critique or criticize, and I have thoroughly enjoyed the naive and simple just as much as the more complex and profound.

I hope you enjoy this book as much as I have enjoyed putting it together, and if you want to know a little more about any of the writers featured, there is a short biography of most of them at the back of the book or online at www.CollectionsofPoetryandProse.com.

Best wishes and lots of **LOVE**!

Robin Barratt
Editor and Publisher

PS: if you want to contribute to any of our forthcoming collections, go to the back of this book!

PPS: Do treat yourself to a copy of LONELY too, and build up your library of our unique book series! Details... yes, at the back of this book too!

LOVE

A Collection of Poetry and Prose
on Loving and Being in Love

When I First Saw You
By *Anonymous*

For Mary J.

When I first saw you,
I just knew
I wanted to spend the rest of my life with you.

I hugged you tight.
I kissed your lips.
Your smile became my smile.
You suddenly became my world,
My joy
My life.

Later, when I kissed you eyes,
and held your face,
and brought you close to me,
and made love to you.
I knew I was yours forever.
And you were mine.

I love you,
with all my heart.

Today
By Rachel Walker

We wake up one morning, all tangled limbs and hair. Arm wrapped around my shoulder, stubble scratching my cheek. Dusty sun slips under the rose patterned curtains and its golden shadows creep across the duvet. I cough slightly and grab my phone, bleary eyes scouring listless Facebook posts as I gently accustom myself to the world. He squeezes me tighter, a sudden surge of warmth.

We talk about the night before, my stomach queasy as I recall. Skinny chips and cheese, jelly shots that wouldn't budge, a lot of Arctic Monkeys and jokey dancing. Analyse bits and pieces of his friends' behaviour: the one who won't shut up, the one whose girlfriend dictates his every move. When did we leave? Do you remember the last song? Conspiratorial tone and laziness; a laughing reluctance to disentangle.

Dark streaks of eyeliner smudge my face as I finally get up. He brings me breakfast in a chipped red bowl; a ham and cheese toastie oozing cheddar, leaving a dizzy spray of crumbs. A bit of TV, maybe, a film later. We can never decide on what to watch on Netflix: I like glossy period dramas and ditzy romantic films, but he'd rather watch a comedy, something mindless but witty. We always compromise though, and are surprised by what we like.

No flatmates, thankfully, not until tomorrow. There's a certain sprawling luxury about having a house all to yourself. But we decide to go for a walk: the sky is cornflower and the grass gleaming, and he knows a picturesque route by the river. We fall to reminiscing. Our first date, four years before, in a small but prettily decorated café. Scones smeared with apricot jam and steaming hot tea, delivered in delicate china cups by a beaming waitress. Then the day he asked to be his girlfriend, huddling in the worn doorway to escape the plummeting forceful rain. We tried to kiss in the rain, later, but it's not as romantic as people think: slippery and wet, shivering as noses bump awkwardly, the rain plopping on shiny foreheads. And our first holiday, to Greece: bursts of vibrant floral colour sitting against terracotta stone churches, tacky signs advertising half pizza, half chips for four euros, meandering alleyways leaning down to the glittering and ramshackle sea.

All so lovely. Wandering along, hand in hand, occasional swift clumsy kisses. We sit on a bench, inscribed with a touching message to a deceased wife, watching as dogs narrowly avoid biting each other, as toddlers scramble away from their parents, as couples like us walk smiling.

Then we head to the supermarket. Rows and rows of food,

insatiable choices. I choose mangos and pineapple, and we amble back to his, with armfuls of plastic bags, an exciting novelty to someone who still lives at home. Everything is exciting, though; we feel like a real couple, living together, unpacking groceries, pouring the steaming hot water out from the cramped tortellini. After years of snatched evenings after work, yawning drives home across the motorway – weekends together are both extravagance and normality, a chance to be together in ease and quietness.

Love
By Andrew Hunter

The heart
is a strange muscle

It beats

us up

Fifty Years
By Brian Langley

Was fifty years ago it was, when in the church I stood
And said "I do" when asked if I, forsaking others would,
Take you, my dear, to be my wife, in sickness and in health;
Forever, till the end of time, in poverty or wealth.

Then she was asked the question, like me, she said, "I do;"
Then it was time to kiss the bride - that was the part we knew.
Then sign the book and we were wed, her name, she'd signed away;
We'd started on our voyage that's got us here today.

There's some who said it wouldn't last, we were too young to wed;
That it was just a brief romance, a year or two they said.
A year or two! it's fifty now. There's been some ups and downs,
Times of smiles and laughter and times of tears and frowns.

For life deals up some problems to see if we can cope;
We'd strength to overcome them and not to give up hope.
We've watched our kids mature and grow, have families of their own;
They've most of them inherited the values that we've shown.

Like sharing life together, not quitting when it's rough,
Dividing labour fairly; it's pretty heavy stuff.
We agree on major issues, We have no "mine and yours,"
We do not carry grudges - But I still open doors.

We accept each other's failings, our own, we try to mend.
We share expenses evenly, agree on what to spend.
Walk hand-in-hand when shopping and cuddle when it's cold;
We're friends. companions, lovers; will still be when we're old.

We've spent some years with work and toil as children came and grew,
But as they went their separate ways we tried directions new.
We've travelled far across this land, been overseas as well.
Watched nature at its wond'rous best, wherever 'tis we dwell.

We've camped beside the oceans edge where balmy breezes blow,
We've sat and watched the stars at night, lit only by their glow.
Our hobbies and our interests have, part of our lives become;
We're both involved in running things, not passengers like some

*****

It's time I stopped my rambling, I do it now and then;
And get back to the reason that I picked up my pen;
For now we're in our senior years, our family wandering far,
It's mostly just the two of us, that's how things often are.

And you my love, our children's mum, now fifty years my wife;
You've always been, and will be, the best part of my life.
I loved you back when we were wed, when vows we both exchanged,
And still my love continues, perhaps a little changed.

Back then I called you beautiful, but every year I find
The beauty word's not good enough, now stunning comes to mind.
So there I end my ditty, of fifty years I've told;
I hope there's many more to come, as slowly we get old.

Previously published 2012 in *You Could Write a Poem About That*

Love
By Dayle Ashton

It is waking every morning
With you running through my mind,
It is thinking 'bout the things you said,
It is always being kind,
It is being there to hold your hand,
To help you get across,
It is sharing, it is giving,
It is never at a loss,
It's all about the way you are
And all those things you do,
It is fever, it is passion,
It is being close to you,
It is something everlasting
When that first bright flame burns low,
It can come upon you quickly,
It is helping you to grow,
It is choosing to be loving
And opening up your heart,
It is seeing the best and worst in you,
It is together and apart,
It is showing what's inside me
And all I have to give,
It is friendship and desire,
It is learning how to live,
It is finding words to tell you
Just what I'm thinking of,
When it will not let you down
It is love.

Break Out
By Greg Bogaerts

It seemed like I'd always loved her but it seemed as though she'd always be with her boyfriend and I'd never have a chance to tell her how I felt. To let her know how I felt about her would have been enough. To love her for so long was a suffering I'd not looked at honestly.

Its consequences were subterranean the damage was more extensive than I'd acknowledged to myself. It put me off kilter, I was permanently unbalanced in everything I did. Making myself a meal was doing battle on enemy front lines. It meant the likelihood of blood and bruises.

I couldn't sip a glass of red wine without my mouth finding a flaw in the glass. Only when I wiped my mouth with a serviette and opened it did I see the blot of red humped like a dead animal in the white paper.

I started to dread seeing her out on the town with her boyfriend. Not because she only had eyes for him and barely gave me a glance even though we'd known each other for years. It was her presence that wounded me as surely as if someone had shot me and I'd been fighting forever to recover.

I wondered how long I could go on hurting myself like this because it was me who was responsible for the pain, not her. It was me who couldn't accept that she would probably marry and disappear forever. I wondered whether I loved her or was it an obsession. What is the difference between love and obsession? Not much.

Part of the nature of obsession is not to understand it. It is impossible to put your finger on why a person has such a hold over you. You wonder if it's the flaw in your character that makes you such a captive, a victim. Or whether it's something outside of yourself manipulating your fate because you tell yourself you couldn't possibly be personally responsible for putting yourself through such damnation.

I had to find a cure otherwise the rest of my life would be a sickness of unrequited obsession.

One Friday night I was at a dance at the town hall and she was there drunk. It wasn't the first time I'd seen her like this. Occasionally she seemed to break out. Her face had that look of contrariness that meant she'd do any thing she wanted and if anyone tried to tell her otherwise then she'd do the very thing they were trying to persuade her not to do.

But what I noticed was the look of desperation, fatigue on the face of her boyfriend, as though something had broken in him long ago. I could see he was caught between living alone or staying with her in a state of perpetual unease. Not knowing when she might do when she'd been drinking and was beyond reason.

Drunk, she wouldn't have anything to do with her boyfriend, I watched him scuttle about after her trying to reason with her. He wanted her under lock and key for her own protection, for his sanity.

No one knew, least of all her, what she might do until the moment came upon her. We didn't have to wait long. She stormed away from the boyfriend, up the white marble steps of the town hall heading for the dance floor. Just as she reached the first landing she slipped, her boyfriend was trotting up the stairs behind her carrying her shoes.

He watched as she flayed her arms trying to right herself in mid air, scramble back to the marble landing. She fell backwards through the air, the strobe lights of the dance floor nicking her face with shadow bruises.

But she fell with such grace, such poise you'd have thought she was doing it on purpose. The smack of flesh on marble was so loud the thump of the feet of the dancers paused, then began again.

People came from everywhere as she lay on her back. They crowded around her extended arms to help her up. Soft words came from men and women. But she was having none of it shaking off the ministering hands striding off leaving them standing there.

As she passed me with a belligerent glare, I looked closely at her, there wasn't a mark on her to be seen, nothing to indicate any sort of injury at all. She kept going and I heard some of the people, who'd come to her aid, begin to weep softly as if they wanted to hide their pain and their confusion.

But I understood as the boy friend walked past me and gave me a wry grin as if to say it's always like this but what can you do. I knew what to do, I went home and got the first good night's sleep I'd had in years. Her fall was deliverance for me because her ruthlessness with others, her animal stamina, her ability to side step pain while others suffered for her, scared me.

I started driving cabs with a sane madness, hour after hour until her form became less than a memory.

Empty Rooms
By Maxine Rose Munro

This is my place, here I feel safe.
In a cocoon of our life together.
Shelves of books, tastes grown
closer over the years, a bed we
bought together and moved
from house to house to here.
It smells of us, I smell of you,
and when you are not home
I roam from room to room to
room, not restless but content.
Like the hermit crab's shell, this
place is our protection, together
we melded and together we are.

Love Haiku
By Kimmy Alan

I'm in love with you
If only you would love me too
Hearts forever fused

Wedding
By Kirsty A. Niven

Inside, the dim chatter of hushed voices
echo outside our encased bubble;
blocking out their awed eyes
as we stand with clasped hands.

Vows are absorbed into the very universe,
reverberating through the timelines.
Molten tears trickle down cheeks,
embracing the salty Blacksmith's floor.

Our gazes irrevocably tied,
golden rings passed on from grandparents
take their place, a new appendage
vital as an organ transplant.

Flashes and clicks blur around us,
our hands still bound, eyes still fastened –
as long as we both shall live.

Is This Love?
By Pamela Scott

Is this love?
These feelings for you,
the thoughts I have
and things I want.
From the first moment
it was like we were meant to be.
I stepped into your arms
and stopped being afraid.

You looked at me
like no one ever had before,
like you really saw me
and liked me just fine.
Dancing in your arms that night
caused all my hidden fears to vanish.
You made me not afraid
to be myself and no one else.

No one has ever touched me
the way you do, with such loving
tenderness, like I am a fragile
piece of glass you fear breaking.
No one has ever looked at me
the way you do with such hunger
in their eyes, with such lust
or such affection.

You make me hurt
in all the right places.
You make me smile
in all my secret spots.
You make me feel
more alive than I thought possible.
happier than I realised I could be
and more desirable than I knew I was.

We fit each other so perfectly
you'd think we were meant to be.
You fit my arms so well you'd
think they were born to hold you.
You get me

and no one ever has
You understand me
like no one else.

Sometimes when you look at me
I feel like the most beautiful woman
on earth. Sometimes when you
look at me I can't breathe.
You share this crazy wavelength
and are on the same wacky page.
You catch my drift
and understand every word I say.

You make me feel safe
like you'll always be by my side.
You make it all better
and the world seems less scary.
When you kiss me
everything around vanishes,
and the only thing that's real
is the feel of your lips on mine.

When you hold me
I never want you to let me go.
I want you to hold me forever
and stop me from shaking.
When you smile at me
the strength runs from my legs
My heart starts to flutter
and I want to worship you.

When you touch me
I want to melt under your
gentle hands. My skin shudders
and I completely lose control.
When we make love
I never want it to end.
I want to touch you forever
and forget everything else.

No one has ever wanted me
the way you do,
with such intensity
and pure passion.
You make me feel

like I've never felt before
and never will again,
as long as I live.

You make me feel like
I am good enough,
and I've never had
that feeling before.
You make me feel
like everything will be okay,
and no one will hurt me again
as long as you are by my side.

You make me believe
in things I thought were myths,
in my own abilities
and my self-worth.
You make me want
to dance naked in the rain,
climb on a roof during a thunderstorm
and cry tears of happiness.

Is this love?
My pounding heart,
the way you make me shudder
and how you make my heart sing.

Is this love?
The way you see through
all my layers of self defence
with just one look.

Is this love?
The way you make me drop my
guard with so little effort.
My barriers crumble around you.

Is this love?
The way you do the things you do,
that makes me smile secretly to myself
and keep me awake at night.

Is this love?
The way you touch me
like I've never been touched before,

and make me shiver with delight.

Is this love?
The way I always think of you.
No matter what I'm doing
your face is always in my mind.

Is this love?
You bring out my wild side,
my dangerous side and the part
of me that craves adventure.

Is this love?
And if it is
why am I so afraid?
Why do I cry when I'm alone?

I have periods of happiness
entwined with bouts of crying.
One minute I'm on top of the world,
the next I'm so scared I can't move.
Deep fear grips me in the dead of night
when I imagine waking up
to discover this is all a dream,
and you don't exist anymore.

I'm so afraid to love you
but I'm more afraid to lose.
I'm terrified to trust you
in case you break my heart.
I never thought I could feel like this
about another human being.
I didn't think anything in me
was capable of such intensity.

I've never loved anyone or anything
in my whole life but I think I love
you, which makes me
scared of something.
I had such a sentimental idea
about love. I thought it was all roses
and sunshine, thunder and lightning
and brilliant fireworks.

I thought I would know love when

I saw it, I would feel it coming from
miles away, that it would be so loud
it would drown everything out.
I never thought love could be so quiet
that it could creep up on you
without making a sound,
and kiss you in the dark.

I never thought love could be so
calm, so still and soothing,
so tender and gentle
and as light as a feather.
I didn't think love was so huge
without a beginning or an end,
without thought or reason
and could go on forever.

I'm addicted to you
like something I can't get enough
of. One taste is not enough. My
thirst for you will never quench.
When you take my hand in yours
I never want you to let it go.
I want to hold you forever
until nothing matters but us.

You have captivated my heart
and soul, making them dance to
your tune. You can bend my heart
to your will and make me whole.
I think I love you.
Deep down inside I know that I do.
I love you
but I'm terrified.

Loving you terrifies me.
It means giving you power over
me, letting you into parts of me
I've long lost the keys to open.
It means ripping bandages off
old wounds and making them
bleed again, facing up to a past
I've been running from forever.

I gave you the knife in my heart

and you removed it with ease,
stopped the bleeding with a soft
hand, kissed the wound closed.
I'm so afraid to love you
and feel something so huge.
To drop my coat of armour
and completely expose myself.

I'm so vulnerable around you
like a little girl in grave danger,
who does what she must even
if there will be harm done.
Is this love?
And if it is
what am I supposed
to do now...?

The Temple
By Pab Roberts

In India, when I was young, a laced-up collar and a new-spiced bun were the things I treasured most. Not Karole, my half-sister whom I despised; nor strawberry laces, which all the British kids seemed to covet when I first came here to school. I have never understood the appeal of these factory-boiled sweets, these fake imitations of enjoyment where fresh and handmade are a possibility. You will be relieved, perhaps, to know that I now value my sister more than I did then. In fact I have to say that Karole is my saving grace, whenever I have been at one of life's many crossroads, she has been there to steer me away from the dangers and show me the way forwards. We may not live in the same continent even but she is with me in so very many ways.

Granny-gee's cooking was always a delight, she used plenty of clarified butter and her sweet baking always had rosewater, she said it had been denied to her by her father until she was nine as he thought her not yet able to appreciate its goodness and that ever since she had been unable to let more than a few days pass without using it in someway or another. Her hair was rinsed in the sweet liquid every day before morning prayer.

I remember peeling the golden layer back off the top of one of her buns, feeling the warm steam caress my cheeks as I uncovered the plump and inviting dough beneath, then hiding in a cupboard up off the first floor balcony, so Karole wouldn't find me and steal my prize. She was a couple of years older than me and these things mattered; in-fact they still matter to this day. I suppose an adult would see the two of us and hypothesise that it were only natural for us not to get-on; her father had died when Karole was two and my mother had been destroyed by fever when I was still in my infancy. Our remaining parents had gotten together for numerous reasons, not least of which being support and shared-loss, and we had stayed apart for numerous reasons of our own. We tolerated each other at mealtimes and family parties but I would not have allowed her my baked sweetmeat for all the tea in the world. Granny-gee would have seen her right anyway; looking back I realise this now. Granny-gee was not my granny, even though I looked upon her as such, Granny-gee was an employee of my father's, yet she was Granny-gee to me and a whole host of kids in the neighbourhood and there were many like me who knew where to get a cuddle and a sugar cube when we scraped our knees in the forested hills around Shimla.

Karole called me from the street, she was bored and I was

her surest playmate. Funny to think we played together so much when we were such sworn combatants. Children have different rules you see. She had discovered a cave up in the hills – or one of her lieutenants had – and we were to explore it. I allowed her to search for me a bit as I devoured my confectionery find and then revealed myself at the top of the stairs like a Mogul Prince greeting his guide. I was six at this point and Karole was nearer eight, only in my mind did I dare think of here as inferior, she would have had me crying 'Uncle' if she had caught a whiff.

    The cave was on a slope located behind the railway bridge. It had not been found by us before because to get to it you had to jump onto the tracks momentarily to access the ridge beyond. As one might imagine, this was agreed as out-of-bounds to we children and it was only because of the exciting prospect of this being a goldmine or a haunted dragon's lair that we plucked-up enough courage to disobey and venture forth. Karole held my hand lest I slip down the incline and, stride by stride, we gained enough height up the slope to disappear from the view of any boatmen on the river below and climb onto the ridge. It was a beautiful yet dreadful sight, the cave had been silent for so long, it was plain to see and whether dragons or gold diggers had been privy to it once, there were now none to be feared. Fronds of native greenery half-obscured the entrance and Karole held these aside so we could look within.

    It looked like a temple had been hewn from the cliffs by a god. Strange faces leered down at us from columns at the side and at the doorstep was a shallow bowl dyed red from what I assumed to be blood offerings. Karole screamed and fell backwards, clutching vainly to the scraggy leaves she held but it was no use, her sandals had twisted about her feet and she was losing balance with every flailing movement. Forgetting about the temple behind us I leapt forwards and wrapped my arms about her waist pulling her back-up to the safety of the cliff wall. Panting, we sat still and cried for a moment, neither of us ready for another loss in our lives. We must have sat there for a half-an-hour or more for we suddenly realised by the hooting of a train approaching that we were getting close to lunchtime. I helped Karole back down the path and we ran for home hand-in-hand, breathless and happy in the sunlight.

    That hillside cave became our place and we would leave messages for each other there whenever one of us had been home for the holidays and the other hadn't. We named it the temple of Shiva and left offerings of incense and dried fruit for him to appease the fear that had sent Karole tumbling that day in June one Summer back when we were children. She never stumbled again but, if she did, I was always ready to catch her.

Love's Transmission
By David Watt

Love has not a boundary, nor limit in extent,
No words to best explain the cause,
Or way to have it sent;
Until the heart receiving is identified as yours,
The precious gift is truly meant,
And each of you adores.

And as such thoughts continue
You will feel love holding sway
In every nerve and sinew,
In each word true lovers say;
Arising deep within you,
Come what will and come what may.

Then each and every second
Will be better than before,
Now love's target has been reckoned,
The destination sure,
Tender feelings beckoned
There to linger evermore.

Love must be treated lightly,
In touch but not in measure;
For its worth is valued rightly
As a guarantee of pleasure,
Contentment dreamt of nightly,
Waking days become as leisure.

My Darling Love
By Jessica L. Jackson

I wondered today when I realized I loved you.
When, I thought? When was it?
Was it when the stars came out for the very first time?
Was that it? Was that when?

Could it be that I have loved you
From the time the sea first kissed the sand?
Was it then? Could it be then?

I remember the time when the mountains formed.
It was before then. Yes, it was.
Do you remember the grass growing between our toes?
It was before that. And even then.

Could it be that I have loved you
From the time that wind commenced to blow?
Was it then? Could it be then?

We spoke of our love as the dawn arrived.
Which dawn? I do not remember.
Was it the dawn when the world began?
No, I loved you before then.

Could it be that I have loved you
From the time flames danced and flickered.
Was it then? Could it be then?

Maybe I should ask when didn't I love you?
When was that? Was there a then?
When I was unloved and you were unloved?
But, there was no then.

For, I realized that I have always loved you.
Forever then,
Forever now,
Forever tomorrow.

Love
By Kathleen Vallance

Love is a look, a touch, a smile,
The encouragement needed for that extra mile.
An intimate moment, or just being a friend;
Love's the foundation on which we depend.

In a world where possessions and riches are sought,
Love is not for sale and cannot be bought.
For sharing, caring and giving's an art,
and love is a gift, a gift of the heart.

Love is there in the warmth of a mother's sweet face,
the mentor, the friend, the teacher of grace.
The buffer against what society breeds,
the sower, the reaper of love's precious seeds.

Love is abundant, but do be aware,
it can be destroyed if not treated with care.
It needs to be nurtured as history records,
a sacrifice worthy of such a reward.

Love was there on the face of the one who was born
to carry the cross, the crown of thorns.
One man, cruelly taken so mankind could live;
two words softly spoken, Father, forgive.

Awakening
By Ryan Joel

Many a night I have spent. My frame hunched over paper or keyboard. Scribbling. Rambling. Many a night I have felt the frustration of nothing. Emptiness. A willing hand but a hollow thought. A battle of wills. To write or not to write?

Although my spirit was willing. My mind refused. It was caught up in the world. Caught up in the noise. The noise distorted everything. Ruined the clarity. Tainted purity. Many a night I switched off that barren screen. Crumpled that starved piece of paper. Cursed my belligerent pen.

Friends urged me on. Write they said. But I knew. I felt like an en engine with no fuel. And I felt spent. Used up and redundant. I could not find the space. That little room in my mind I often retreated to was nowhere to be found. I was floundering in the dark with no light or inkling as to what I was supposed to do or where exactly I needed to go.

Disoriented and anxious. I feverishly tried writing about any little thing that came to mind. But it was no use. It all ended like a really bad lab experiment. Twisted, distorted and damaged. My words contorted into an unrecognisable mass of senseless drivel. I finally closed my laptop for the final time. My mind exhausted. Throbbing from exhaustion. I accepted defeat.

And then you. You with your beautiful words. Your colourful prose. I couldn't. I wouldn't believe it. Try as I did. The echoes of your ghosted words haunted me. Reverberating inside my head. Your gentle tongue mocked them. Played with them. Teased them. And my words and their thoughts were once again full of life and vigor.

The final blow. You laughed. And like a shock-wave it ploughed right through me. Wave after wave. Resonating in every molecule of my existence. And that was it. I could no longer ignore it. A literary geyser had started to erupt. You. You. You. All your doing. All your sincerity. All your kindness. I was ill prepared for this. But well equipped for the result.

I dove for my tools. Like a mad hatter at a tea party. I was like a writer possessed. I scribbled. Typed. Scribbled. Typed some more. The words poured out of me. I was in the throes of my masterpiece. Come to think of it. I still am. I have found my room again. All because of you.

Your smile shone the light. Your words unlocked the door. And you laughter blew away the dust to my chamber. I'm back in my place of wonder. It's musky. It's grotty. Absolutely perfect. And with that. I usher you to a seat beside me. And then our story begins.

Chagall's Village
By Alan Murphy

Locked into
A loving gaze
On this laughing
Carnival
of the heart.

The Perfect Couple
By Katie Lewington

the perfect couple
is
those two singles you see in the background of every quote you
reblog, filter to cover up and brush over
all in a days hard grafting -
like they've never witnessed the sun coming up for air
or sat in the back of a police van

crystals, rough to touch

The perfect couple does not exist
we all embody a breathing cliché that society resists -
age gaps, daddy, same sex

picture doesn't show the real us
anybody can fake a smile to find a mate

Tell Me It's Real
By Molly Donald

This is not a love story.

They are cliché and boring;
whilst we are chaotic and misaligned,
going against the evolving times.
Planets did not fall in formation
for us, we just became our own creation.
I am not the girl-next-door: quietly laughing,
with a pop-band blasting,
and each move as graceful as the last.
My fingernails scratch against the past.
Whispering, I ask,
what's it like on that grass?
Does it feel better than your hair?
Is it as comforting as the chaos in our own air?
No.

This is not a love story.

Life is not simple. I fall into your arms softly,
and the world knocks on me obnoxiously.
Sharp tongues later caress each other's skin.
Apologies for the misdemeanour, I just like to sin.
Each fervent kiss blooms from the unexpected.
The list of movies ending in what we anticipated:
a sigh -
But, why?
I want real.
I demand an idea, and someone, you see,
nobody has had before.
Give me something nobody has yet to explore;
or cried over, into blankets of the box office hits.
I would rather just skip it.
The one about that guy, that girl, and that thing.
It is always something.
That is what a love story is:
Love and it's happily ending bliss.

This is not a love story.

We are both angry at the world.

Tired of running away, like squirrels.
Love is our accessory -
not our tale of victory.
Nick and Norah are not our aspirations,
their cliché is on a screen for a reason.
Before you call this "it", think.
Also, try to sleep for a few winks.
Then, tell me that this is ours.
All of this is our story;
and I am lucky it involves my love for you.
However, this is not a love story.
We are much more than a Hollywood movie.

Love
By Vaijayantee Bhattacharya

Soft kisses of fading winter chill
Glowing red roses in backyards
You spin a yarn of mutable dreams
That melt into void at my finger tips
Yet love is in the air they say
In scarlet hearts of the shopping malls
Like silver bells that tell a tale
As Santa descends in his reindeer cart
Red Santa, red roses, red hearts
Red wounds that turn brown with time
So red you are and yet so blue
So gray perhaps to teary eyes
Yet love it is in all its shades...
Love is blue, red and perhaps gray
And green too at the sapling's edge
And yellow at the birth of dawn
Love perhaps it is of sorts
On which the world tosses around
Love it is that wins the day
The battle lost to cruel time
So love be true, today again
And flawless red like the velvet rose
Bring peace and joy to the heart and hearth
Love in you my little sun grows

Hanging On
By Kathleen Boyle

"Will you three stop fighting,for goodness sake!!" This was mum's signature tune. We never did; stop fighting, that is. We couldn't help it; three kids in a small house; middle of winter; bored to the eyeballs. What else was there to do?

Mum tried her best; Cluedo, Monopoly, Playstation, Sky TV... We had the lot, but no matter what we had to entertain us, when the three of us were together it would always end in a fight. Boys will be boys, and if there's a sister thrown in for good measure, the potential for arguments is immense.

Mum had a very short fuse that winter. She and dad had divorced in the spring of that year; then she lost her job and money became really tight. It was around New Year that her behaviour became very worrying.

She joined a wood-work class. This in itself wasn't a problem; it was when she began using her new skills that I began wondering.

Looking back I suppose we kids had taken advantage of our situation. Mum had grown weary of our constant bickering and began to spend more and more time in her room, away from us. I was the oldest and must admit to noticing the tired, worried expression which had replaced her sunny smiles; but there was fun to be had, and mum, being mum, would soon bounce back, I told myself.

One day after a particularly explosive outburst she retreated into the shed. As we rampaged our way through the day our curiosity was aroused by the sounds of sawing, sanding and hammering.

Mum emerged eventually and locked the door after her.

It was sad to witness her present state. I was old enough to remember the days when our family were as happy as the next. When the arguments began I was puzzled, but eventually their life together was one long row. Mum became worn down by it all and dad found comfort elsewhere. Now it seemed her life was disintegrating, together with the house, furniture and, I suppose, hope.

Two days after the shed episode, mum was summoned to school by my Head-Teacher. I was in trouble, again. I knew it would go down badly, and waited for the onslaught.

Nothing angered her more than school problems; but when she emerged from the Head's office her face was pale and immobile. She walked right past me without a word. We clambered into the car and drove home in silence. At home mum cooked tea, washed up and locked herself in the shed. Of course I knew she was upset and on reflection the silent treatment was a lot worse than rage. I wondered what was going on. She had withdrawn from us and seemed absorbed in her shed project and woodwork lessons. Books had appeared with strange titles; *Do It Yourself Shelving, Hinges and Brackets, Dovetailing for Beginners*, a far cry from mum's usual *Mills and Boon*.

One evening, not long after the school incident, I answered the phone. A strange man's voice asked for mum.

"Who's speaking?" I snooped.

"Constable Metcalf." Came the brusk reply. Stunned, I went to fetch mum, whereupon I was driven out of the room. Mum talked in low, serious tones, then hung up and headed straight for the shed. I began to worry something was terribly wrong. Why was she getting calls from the police? What had she done?

It was early March and the days were lengthening. One afternoon I came home from school to find what looked like a scaffold erected in the garden.

"What's that?" I asked.

"What does it look like?" mum replied. Curtly.

"I know what it looks like mum but what's it for?"

"What do you think?" she snapped, and walked into the house. I was flabbergasted. Had things really got that bad? I knew it had been a horrible year, what with the divorce, school problems, no money and then the business with the police. But surely not!

I followed mum into the house. She was on the phone and hung up hastily. My stomach was churning. "Mum are you OK?"

"Yes, never better." Strange words for mum.

"How about a cup of tea?" I heard myself asking. Mum glanced at me, puzzled.

"Are you OK?"

"Yes of course. We all love you mum. You know that don't you?"

"Well you have a funny way of showing it sometimes," she smiled. "I will have that cuppa though."

I made the tea and sat beside her as we drank. She was smiling for the first time in ages, and it occurred to me that this was probably the first cup of tea anyone had made her since dad left. When she'd finished I took her cup and gave her a big kiss. She beamed, just the way she used to I thought. That's my real mum; she's still there I told myself. I only have to try a little and perhaps she'll come back for good.

At school next day my mind wandered frequently to the gruesome structure in the garden and I was more than a little worried.

Jumping off the school bus, I noticed a police car parked outside our house. I felt sick. This wasn't happening.

My brother and sister ran ahead, excited by the sight of the police-car. I hesitated at the gate. My brother was calling: "Come and see. Come and see!"

Taking my hand he pulled me along to the back of the house. There stood the most beautiful array of hanging baskets, cascading from mum's handiwork.

Mum smiled. "This is Constable Metcalf from my woodwork class. He came to help me fix the frame for the baskets. Do you like them?"

She was beaming radiantly, and as I gushed my admiration, I noticed she slipped her hand into Constable Metcalf's. Mum was back, and everything was going to be fine!

Your Arms Are The Walls
By Courtney Speedy

Your arms are the walls
I need to keep me warm.
So hold me close even
after the rising of dawn.
Let your kisses be firewood
to set the fire in my heart
alight for the cold nights.
Your hands on my hips
keeping me stable in
the frame of your body.
You are the woodwork
that keeps me upright.
Let's let the wind talk
as your hands paint
me in love and strength.
Your hands are a
paintbrush covering
me in love with each
gentle stroke and
letting the fire smoke.
Your eyes are windows
and I can see straight
into your beautiful soul.
Your body is a building
of strength and security
against the harsh weather
and promising me forever.
I feel warmth and love and
know I will never be alone
again because I am deep
inside of your bones and
you are my home.

The Book
By Lonita Nugrahayu

Oh my dear one,
move one...
the life of yours is like a book that has so many chapters,
one chapter has ended,
open the new one.
Your life has not ended yet.

She smiles.
Her fragile smile,
yet sincere one.

She looks above,
searching for someone there,
someone who is very much alive inside her,
yet nowhere to be found.
She looks at me,
with her loveable fragile smile,
and she whispers...
"Love is the life to me,
and he is the love.
By all means, he is the book.
Every chapter in it,
will always has him, always.
I am moving on,
but I don't leave him behind,
because he is the book.
The only book."

Synonym
By Nilanjana Bose

Can't say if he's my north and south, my sea and earth,
but I know he's my compass always pointing true.
He's the track I lose sometimes, he's its frantic search.
The jet contrail aiming home through the clearest blue.

He's the stone fortress and its secret passageway;
the arched roof of tunnels; the stem of the goblet.
He's the fizzing froth of light that makes up the day;
he's that single star improving on the sunset.

Not my working week, no, he's my blessed Sabbath -
the spine of sacredness binding leaves of routine;
he's my quiet street, my escape route, my private booth;
he is my ruby wine, he's my strongest caffeine.

He isn't my voice or tongue, neither a song nor hymn.
He is not life or love. Only their synonym.

Time Heals All
By John R. Sabine

Time heals all, or so they say,
Time to cleanse the hurt and tears;
But will time forever keep at bay
Those memories that fuel my fears?
Is time enough to smooth the rough
Or will it always call my bluff?

Time heals all, or so they tell.
Yet what is time but rate of change
Must I change as well to break that spell,
To bring my senses back in range?
Time cures, I know, it must be so,
How else could I endure the blow.

Time heals all, or so I've heard,
Time to wipe a slate of mem'ries clean;
For time is the cure by all preferred,
To dim those stars my heart has seen.
Of course it's true, I must believe anew,
How else to cure my soul of you?

Previously published 2012. *On Thinking About It*, Ginninderra Press, Port Adelaide, Australia.

Live And Love
By Steve Howrie

The summer's hot, the winter's cold.
And though I age, I don't feel old;
We live and die, and live a-gain,
Through all the years, through all the pain.

The sun goes down, the swallow flies.
A Soul goes home, a baby cries;
We live and die, and live again,
Through all the years, through all the days.

We meet at night, a warm caress
We touch and hold, and both undress;
We live and love, and love again,
Through all the years, through all the nights.

And in the end, I stay with you.
For ever more, a dream come true;
We live and love, two Souls entwined,
Until the end, the end of time.

If I Could
By S'busiso Manqa

If I could, I would -
If I could,
I would pull the moon towards you,
Just to make your darkest days a bit lighter

If I could,
I would change the skies to your liking,
I'd shape the rocks
To pleasure only your eyes

If I could,
I'd rearrange the shores
So the blessings of the waves could come your way

If I could,
I'd explain my love for you in material,
But I'm too afraid it just won't be enough

If could,
I'd call you mine because I'd like to think
No one sees you as a blessing as much as I do

If I could,
I'd leave you without an explanation
Because this effect you have on me is far too great to beat

If I could,
I'd explain your presence in my life as that calling I just can't seem to understand -
The call I fail to pick up

My daily thoughts of you are not of obsession,
But of confusion -
I didn't choose to walk besides you,
I was directed towards you by a force I don't understand -
So please don't blame it on my loneliness that I fell for you

Sometimes I wish I could see you cry - just so I could wipe off your tears slowly and prove how true my love is

I don't know if you're a destination or a map,

I wish I could be more to you -
But I'm afraid it's a danger because I'd be committing to what I don't understand

Your rejection to me after this confession
Will be like a gun shot at the end of an epic scene
Bang Bang -
Just before I die and before you leave me
I've decided to drop my pride
And admit I truly do love you

Black Cream For Ruined Hearts
By David Hollywood

Black cream to soothe...
and smooth, with grace,
An elegance unseen,
Of colours, yet too pale to blush,
Embalmed by darkest touch,
And dyes from out the gash conceal,
The wounds which seep to gush,
Consoled by softest tint reveals...
a screen, too faint to flush,
And kindness that shall shade our flow,
Adorns our dreams of you,
When ashen faint we sense to know,
How vivid tones can show,
A hue disguised by tinges which,
 From now shall cease to glow.

Meeting On The Footpath
By Keith Nunes

Your face broke my heart but I wouldn't go back to you, my new lover held my hand tightly, the three of us motionless on the footpath in a town, any town where lovers effortlessly crush each other, I felt like an assassin who had just killed your two children with a fish boner, my girlfriend said something that included my name, we moved around you but you stared ahead, I watched over my shoulder as you fell to your knees and put your face in your hands.

Llandudno Pier
By Andrew Hunter

Wish you were here
I need you now

Wish you were here
I don't know how

to find the words
this far from home

I wish...
        ...alone

Kasia By The Seashore
By Marc Brightside

The eleven-twenty-seven came without applause;
Bournemouth has the nicest beaches,
so I was told, but I needed an excuse.
Plenty of Fish provided one. We met
at an aquarium and sped through introductions
cooing over penguins in the South West sun,
stupid and young, an afternoon accredited
to Kasia By The Seashore. I never called her that
aloud. Perhaps I should have. Our kiss was
an appalling cliché, two strangers by the bridge
at midnight, and her heartbeat quivered
through her neck into my fingers. "Do you have to go?"
she asked. "I don't know, do I?" We fucked
to Billy Joel, The Raconteurs, some other band
I can't recall and texted through the week,
where full-stops faded into colons and
parentheses. "I'm going away," I told her,
some time down the line, "for a research trip
in Holland." Because that's what real writers do,
they go on research trips. "I'll still be here
when you get back," she said, "bring some pictures
home, okay?" I never showed her any photographs.

Be It Your Love Is Gold
By Pallang Mofokeng

Call me not be it your love is gold,
Absent me from your raging sentiment so cold.
Love is Anathema, whose roots are pleasures
Not to incline but be spent beyond measures.

No. No! No! sense of it all,
Is life so on the roll.
But dear Princess neglect me not, when I utter 'No
inclination help won't be gold'
Love is not silver nor can you fake it gold.

Roses are precious to give, a pleasure for them who receive
But woe they be deceived!
Love's named romanticism bared by givers who give
Yet love's far a mystery from romantic gifts, she is
beyond what men can give.

Call me not be it your Zest is gold
Love is silver, love is stars in this world so cold...

One Word Only
By Sara Spivey

I caught a glimpse of myself in the mirror. With droplets of luke warm water slowly dripping from my chin I didn't recognise myself any longer. The woman looking back had a warmth in her eyes and an ease of expression on her full mouth. The hair was scruffy and thrown up on top and held in place with a chopstick. Certainly a few pounds could be lost but she was definitely comfortable with herself.

This conquest only took 37 years I mused. Sarcasm aside, why now?

I vaguely recalled an occasion tugging at the ropes of my memory, waiting in the wings to enter centre stage. As I gently cajoled it awake it freshened quickly and I smiled faintly.

At a dinner party years earlier a puzzle had been posed by a vivacious business woman, strong and confident of character. The guests were challenged to find the definition of several words. However, the difficult part, she enunciated in her affected London tone, you could only answer with one word. She purred with subtle amusement as she delivered them. Your definition of happiness – in one word, your definition of success in one word, and finally – your definition of love in one word, of course.

Well the dinner guests were all a titter at this, how entertaining they chimed. They all raised their wine glasses to this frivolous game and hunkered up their courage to answer with another gulp of the grape juice.

The first to volunteer, a suited man, late 30s, media-type who always landed the deal, was eager for his gravelly lilt to be heard above and before the others. Showing his command and lack of fear of judgement. Plain arrogant to be honest.

Success, 'Obviously that's money' he guffawed. Straight onto happiness, 'That's easy too', he flicked his ash lazily into the silver spoon next to his plate before offering his verdict – 'Fame'. Then came the love question. He faltered. He opened his mouth then snapped it shut again. He twitched a crooked smile and still nothing came.

Another man, salt and pepper hair on the opposite side of the table tried to rattle him. 'Ooh Jeremy' he had boomed, 'This one got you scuppered old chap?'

With another tap on his cigarette Jeremy simply announced, 'Sex'. Now everyone chuckled or heckled, mainly to cover up their opinion of how obtuse Jeremy was. However, by the looks now hovering around the beautifully laid table, the desperate racking of brains was afoot.

Given the confines of a plush social gathering of a dear friend, fuelled by plenty of jovial banter and chinking of crystal, cigarette smoke and satiated stomachs, ones psyche was having a tough time harnessing this seemingly fun-filled quiz. One word just didn't seem to provide justice or explanation to one's rationale.

Our verbal responses bore open wells to our innermost souls, places that even intimate acquaintances were often denied access.

Next, our host had rounded on me. I remembered briefly blushing, rapidly composed myself, bought a second or two by clearing my throat. I had looked up from under my eyelashes, smiled a half smile to elicit confidence from my peers and continued.

I carefully picked happiness as my answer to success. Cockily my ego scoffed that I sounded so evolved. A little more tricky was happiness. Whilst Jeremy had been performing I had come up with my theory on this, then countered it. It sounded boring but when processed internally, for me, it was the accurate response. Con...tent...ment. I eased the word out slowly and syllable by syllable quickly flashing a look around the table attempting to interpret their feedback.

There were slow thoughtful nods and grunts of agreement as realisation was settling in. Then here it was... love. A thousand images had come crashing into and out of my conscious thought, mulling all of them over for a few split seconds. I only had this one word that came and came again knocking for my approval. With a small flick of my head I smiled broadly now, voice light and firm, 'Unconditional'.

What a tantalising game, totally engrossing, superficially humorous but emotionally and intellectually tormenting. We were later told amongst much gossip, laughter and soul searching how our answers would change over time.

It was true, mine had been refined and now, this morning, I believe I had arrived at my final destination. Back to the most difficult of them, love. I rubbed the smudge of toothpaste away, winked and delivered my final answer. 'ME!'

My Love
By Akwu Sunday Victor

Just came to mind, the days I spent
Thinking and wondering upon your state my state
My heart was clothed with the cloud

My heart was clothed with the clouds
And all night long cried out loud for love
My heart was clothed with the cloud

My love for her was thicker than the stem of an Iroko
It flowed through the stream-path of my heart
My heart was clothed with the cloud

I could hear the birds singing in the woods
I could hear the cackling of the leaves caressed of the wind
My heart was clothed with the cloud

I saw a rainbow appeared in the thick clouds
Fingers from one end of the earth to the other end
My heart was clothed with the cloud

I was waiting for rain to begin falling
And the fruits buried in the draught baked earth to sprout
My heart was clothed with the cloud

I went to bed to sleep, I closed my eyes and was gone
Then in a nightmare, I saw a swam of vultures with bloody beaks
My heart was clothed with the cloud

They began singing, 'we love you as they loved you
That, buried in you is all we want and northing else'
My heart was clothed with the cloud

They clawed the earth and pulled out tender blades
They pulled out sprouting seeds, even the ones dead
My heart was clothed with the cloud

For the love of yesterday's, today's and tomorrow's seeds
They clawed the earth, air, sea and dark places
My heart was clothed with the cloud

My heart was clothed with the cloud

And I anticipated showering my love showers of love
My heart was clothed with the cloud

But now I don't know what has happened to the clouds
Now I don't understand the eerie cries of misery I hear
From lips inflation-battered, and brows poverty-mangled

Midnight Stroll By The Canal
By Pamela Scott

We link hands, cross the
bridge over the canal, rippling in the dark.
We stand for a moment, look over,
and watch the water run under our feet.

We sway against each other,
your hand brushes mine, I shiver.

I love this spot at night,
so peaceful it leaves me speechless.

We walk along the side
of the canal, hand in hand. We talk.

This is our spot, filled with magic.
We're alone in the world,
no-one around for miles.

This place belongs to you and me.

I fell in love with you walking by the canal.
I saw how animated your face was in the moonlight
and how alive the fresh air made you.

We pause to look at the ducks and swans
as they glide through the dark water.

My love for you's grown since our first walk,
now love fills up my lungs and the air around me.

We reach our spot – a concrete seat at the edge of the canal
and sit down. We lean against each other.

This place feels so still and peaceful,
perfectly content and at ease.

I rest my head on your shoulder,
fill my nostrils with your scent
and watch the swans dance in the dark.

Organising Functions And Principles Of Love
By Ian McKenzie

This agonising possibility is undermining my idea of romance as I understood it,
I am understanding all too late,

How unnecessary it is to imagine your love as some perfect hallowed cloister,
Reserved only for those who have forsaken the world and chosen to be your willing oblate.

I learn that your love is not earned by grand acts of surrender or endless rituals of intimate and sacred unction,
Nor by the formulaic recantation of past loves and adolescent sin,
But who,

Who will take the recycling waste out to the wheelie bin?

The Breakup
By Ronald L Kundinger

just a little something
for the pain, she says
(it hurts less when she whispers)
just a cut
a little stab
that bleeds you out
her caress peels flesh
her tongue
lays you open to the bone
naked as Eve
she cups your heart like an apple
grins at you like a starving child
how about one for the road? she asks
your tongue
has been shredded
hush, she says
hush
this won't hurt a bit

The Love For My Niece
By Heidi Al Khajah

I understand you
Not many do
It's a funny thing
Miss chatterbox
Speaking volumes
Not saying a word
You're a bit of me
I'm a bit of you

But auntie I have a voice
I cannot use
It's shut out
And I try, but only lose

Mary it's OK
I've been here before
You're my mini me I'm afraid
And I'll see you through

Put your palm against mine
And let your voice come through
Don't let this shyness
Stop you from being you

You're too much like me
But you'll overcome
The good thing is
You're a bit of me
And I'm a bit of you
And that strength will come too

And Mary
I'll love you always
And like me you will be
Strong
Vibrant and
Free

The Extraordinary Love Poem
By Kariuki wa Nyamu

Love, today I pen you a poem
albeit a plain one,
a poem that wouldn't employ images
for our love is altogether unimaginable.
A poem free of hyperbole

for our love doesn't deserve any extravagant exaggeration.
A poem devoid of metaphors and similes
for our love has got no comparison.

> Love, I pen you
> a poem without personification
>
> for our love will never be inanimate.
> A poem empty of oxymoron and paradox
>   for our love is not at all self-contradictory.
> A poem lacking symbols
> for never will our love signify something else.
>
> A poem with not as many rhetorical questions, since
> where's that time to invest in questions that induce no reply?
>
> Yes, I'll just pen you a device-less poem
> for it's utterly immaterial to conceal our love
> behind any one poetic device!

Love, today I just want to let you know
that you're the love of my life

You who opaque one and all
the irresistibly charming belle
and sole conqueror of my heart's pride!

> So Love, kindly appreciate this extraordinary love poem
>
> for ours is totally out-of-the-ordinary love
>
> since not even the authority of these poetic words
> that I soooo much economize
> can effectively express our immense affection

that'll forever remain remarkably unusual!

First published in *Best New African Poets 2015 Anthology*

Love. Full Stop
By Mandy Mullen.

Love will find a way,
save the day,
brighten your way.
Love will take you to 'EUPHORIA ',
take you to 'DESPAIR.'
It can raise you to the heavens,
can paralyse you on the floor.
Love can find you in 'tip-top' condition,
or in an asylum of delirium and insanity.
Love will course through your veins like an iron rich river,
strengthen your bones with calcified steel.
It will tear your nerves like a paper shredder,
give you pain with no antidote or cure.
Love will support you when you wobble like a jelly,
'take you down' like a sniper's rifle.
It will say "hello" when you least expect it,
say goodbye just the same.
Love will be your hero when you need rescued,
your friend when you just need.
It will blossom like a flower in Spring,
or wither like the autumnal leaf.
Love will surround you with comfort and warmth,
or 'freeze you out' in isolation and loneliness.
Love will ask you 'out to play',
or tell you "go away."
It will 'signpost' the way ahead
or steer you off the 'right path.'
Love will welcome you with open arms
or close the door in your face.
Love is honest, not deceitful,
kind not cruel.
It is an adventure, a mystery tour,
not a dead end.
Love can start war,
bring peace,
create disharmony or joy.
It will 'open the door,'
'seize the day,'
make a man sway.
Love can make you 'drunk' with happiness
or it can 'sober you up' in a sec.

It can make you do
silly things,
spontaneous things,
impulsive things,
foolish things.
It can make you jump up and down,
birl round about,
make you dizzy and daft,
laugh really loud.
Love is loyal and trustworthy
forgiving and kind,
no cheating,
no lies,
no doubt in your mind.
Love does not blame or find fault,
any problems worked out.
Love will kiss you
"Good Morning,"
kiss you
"Goodnight,"
cuddle, caress you,
tell you everything's alright.
It will allow 'freedom of speech,'
not muffle or gag,
dispels disillusion,
pull rabbit from bag.
Love will an air-balloon lift,
the race pistol to start,
butterflies in your tummy,
a faster beat to your heart.
It will build you right up
or tear you right down,
It will cause you to smile
as well as to frown.
Poets have wrote about it,
minstrels have sang,
sirs having duelled over it,
murderers hanged.
A world
without love,
unimaginable I think,
'falling' in it as easy as a 'nod and a wink' !

A Love That's True
By Frank Cardiff

I have sat and watched the dripping of a dewdrop
I have listened to the cold crisp crunch of snow
I have felt the soft caressing of the breezes
And I've wondered where the rainbow's colours go.

I have seen the leaves of Autumn change their colours
I have watched the clouds drift slowly in the sky
I have seen the lightning flash across the heavens
And I sometimes rather vaguely wonder why.

I have watched the gentle lustre of a moonbeam
I have seen the night turn slowly into day
I have listened to the silence and the stillness
And it's then I think I somehow sort of pray.

I've appreciated loyalty and kindness
And I know there is a guiding force above
And I hope my master knows I try to please him
For there's nothing quite as true as puppy love.

Previously published in *The Accidental Poet* (ISBN 978-0-99411944-0-4)

Compare You To A Rose
By David Watt

Compare you to a rose, I can't
For roses bloom and fade away.
Your beauty pays no heed to time
And blossoms new each day.
Your smile makes even sun ashamed
In competition with your gaze.
No warmth was ever stronger felt,
Nor more certain to amaze.
Your hair falls long and graceful -
No artist's brush has mastered yet.
It frames a picture perfect formed
Of beauty delicate.
You move like gentle breezes -
Soft flowing, smooth and free.
Not knowing how you captivate
Each sense inside of me.
Your eyes reflect in China blue
As sunlight strikes your hair.
A portrait lovely, tender, sweet,
Mere words could never share.

He Is
By Kirsty A. Niven

Kaleidoscope-eyed, bubbling with love,
the elevator to God, the lungs in my chest
and forever smiling like the Cheshire cat.

Master of the keyboard, craftsman of metre,
winged with words, a heart-breaker with lines
and always has a compliment to hand.

Angelic, soaring leagues above,
followed by a golden halo at all times,
and causing my heart to flutter.

A Little Tin
By John Stockdill

My little oval window looks right down into their yard. You should come over and take a look for yourself, Maureen. You'd think they would close those Venetian blinds. Parading around the place without a stitch on, I've seen her dancing like that. Handsome woman, I'll give her that much.

The old Australian, she stares. At night, I see her cigarette glow in that little wooden caravan. Watching us. Once I see her down at the fence, and I smile. She scurries off, like a wounded animal. Next day she throws a little tin over the fence. I walk over, carefully I pick it up. Inside, a note: "Piss off back to your jungle."

Such scorn. My Eduardo says he will put her in a pine box. I say don't bother, she's already in one.

Sunday morning there was a piece of paper poked under my door, though I never heard anything in the night. Do you know what it said Maureen?

"Together you and I will dance naked on a cloud. I love you."

I don't know what the hell to make of that, I surely don't. It gave me the creeps. I can't sleep. Maureen I've got to hang up, got them chest pains.

I sent the old one a note back, only kind words. You can get to the very heart of a person with just one sentence, I have always believed this. Now, no more cigarette glowing in the window. For over one week now, nothing.

The Colour Of Love
By Clement Clark

My heart what do you mean
When drip-drip you beatin',
Such joy and pain I'm feelin'
When of this lady I'm thinkin',
My mind is filled with pictures
Of good and everlasting pleasures,
A thought of her in public makes me grin
Passersby look at me asif I'm insane,
Every romantic song that I hear
Brings effervescent feelings of her,
I perform like an utter brat
When in her presence I'm at,
Just picturing her I confess
Fills my belly and I eat less,
At night I sleep not a wink
For it's of her that I think,
My attire has become such a mock
Cos all I wear is colour block,
In her presence my speech sounds silly
I sometimes hate myself for being dilly,
What my heart do you mean?
When drip-drip you beatin',
And 'tis only her I think of
Could this be the colour of love?

Lasting Love
By Jennifer Riggs

Living in tandem:
Living in gear,
Synchronised heart-beat
Synchronised year.
Empathic rhythm
Simpatico mind,
Harmony always:
Two of a kind.

But living is random:
Slipping a gear,
Missing a heart-beat,
Shedding a tear;
Not made in Heaven,
But here, on the earth,
Hard, messy labour is needed for birth.

Alison's Whispers
By Keith Nunes

The policeman asked me if I had known Alison long. "Not really," I said standing in the kitchen with a cup of instant in hand. "Maybe three months. We met at the local pub. She seemed vulnerable, or sort of depressed - but that's an overworked word these days.

"I'd come from living with a boisterous woman and Alison seemed a much better fit with my tone of life. She was lovely, you know, just genuinely gentle... and feminine although she could give you a sharp lip when she felt like it. I think we both felt bashed by life... a little nervous, anxious sort of thing. I was living at the motor camp and she said to move into her wee cabin after a few days of seeing each other. I felt safe... just free to be as quiet and withdrawn as I liked. I guess it was wonderful. But really, I always felt she'd fall too far one day and do something about it."

The funeral was funky - the alternatives took it as a chance to feel 'out' and 'together'. I live in her cabin now. The guy who owned it died and no-one turned up to claim it so there's no rent to pay. This place feels like Alison - it's her whispering to me in the cool of the pristine mornings. I'll never leave.

Weary-eyed Wanderers
By Jenna Rainey

Star-crossed lovers is too cliché, as weary-eyed wanderers together we stray. Through life's daily battles we struggle and conquer, each one a milestone which leads to another. When emotions are rife and we act out of character, opinions soon waver, divided against one another. A tackle ensues when silence proves all too much, wounded in battle we strive forward and touch. Our guards begin to weaken, our judgement now clouded, reconciling follows and our love is re-founded.

Broken Promises
By Farha A. Jaleel

I have always been left out,
never felt loved,
Always hoped for the day,
when I'd be noticed by someone.

Never felt like I belonged.
All I ever wanted,
was someone's love and care.

Then I saw you, that day;
with a smile on your face,
so casual, so carefree.
And I couldn't stop myself,
from falling for you.

Always loved you from the shadows;
never saying a word.
But then you found out
and accepted me for who I was.

Your words,
your honesty,
made me trust you;
and had me falling in deeper.

And when we were wedded,
I thought I'd finally found,
what I'd always wanted
a place where I belonged.

And I never anticipated,
that things would go wrong.
I never saw it coming.

Everything that you kept from me,
all the secrets you didn't reveal,
until later...

All the sadness,
All the pain and insult,
that I bore alone,

at the hands from your family.

But you never did believe me.

I loved you with all my heart.
And, I thought you did too.
Or was it just me all along?
Was it all just to prove a point?

Now, years have gone by,
as I look back,
at all the memories we made;
all the letters you wrote; and wonder;
Did those promises mean anything at all?
Or were they just words to you?

I look back now,
and I know,
I still love the man,
I knew back then;
when we first met...

Bound by Thread
By Jacky Perez

I stared in horror at the broken needle lying near my desk. *Where is the other half?* I frantically searched my desk for the other piece - the end that I knew I had left with thread still attached. I distinctly remembered leaving it by my keyboard after sewing up the blanket that my new puppy had happily torn into the night before. *Maybe I accidentally broke it and the other half is somewhere on my desk.* Still optimistic, I lifted everything off my desk one at a time—the keyboard, the mouse, my papers - looking desperately for the other end of the needle.

I shook my head in disbelief and turned to my 10-pound solid white puppy lying happily in her kennel. "Sue… Did you eat the needle?" I asked her, knowing full well that she couldn't tell me. She looked at me in idle curiosity and turned to a chew toy that was propped up next to her. While she figured out how to hold it between it between her front paws, I returned to my search.

Maybe I imagined I left it on my desk, but actually left it in the blanket. Convinced I was right, I grabbed the blanket I had been working on. I ran my hands over the blanket, hoping that the rest of the needle had somehow entangled itself in it and that I would soon feel it prick my finger. I tried to keep calm but when my hands remained unscathed, I became frustrated and began to crush the blanket. Fistful by fistful, I squeezed the entire blanket to no avail. Exasperated, I tossed it into the kitchen.

Anxiety began to make my stomach knot up, but the the needle had to be lying around somewhere. I dropped to my hands and knees and began to slowly scour the laminate floor of my small studio apartment. For thirty minutes, I searched every inch in my 200 sq. ft. studio apartment for a clue about the needle's whereabouts: a piece of thread, a glint of metal, *anything!*

Tears of frustration began to fill my eyes when I couldn't find a trace of it. I looked in disbelief at Sue. *Why in the world would you eat a needle?* Scared of what the dangers might be for eating a needle, I hopped online to find out what I should do. Not surprisingly, I found a plethora of information and advice about puppies eating things they shouldn't - needles included - and they all said the same thing: go to a vet, immediately!

Luckily, it was Saturday morning and the vet was still open. I rushed over, frantic to get my puppy taken care of. Thirty minutes and three x-rays later, my fears were confirmed.

I stood in front of the vet with Sue Jung lying on the platform table. The vet held up a picture of an x-ray for me to look at it. I stared at it blankly.

"As you can see, she ate the needle." His accusation felt like a direct attack and my poor puppy-parenting.

I stammered in disbelief, "I thought I was careful. It was on my desk. I don't know how she got it."

He ignored my apology and continued on, "There are two other metal pieces in her belly." He held up another x-ray and pointed to some other gray masses that I had thought were food.

"What?!" I was dumbfounded, "I got her from a shady shelter two weeks ago - maybe she ate it there."

He gave me a look that clearly indicated that he didn't believe me. "It's good you caught this before it passed out of her stomach, but this is very dangerous. A needle can go through the dog's intestines, causing internal bleeding, other complications, and it can be fatal."

I nodded my head in agreement, eyes downcast.

He continued, "We can remove these pieces with surgery, but this surgery is very hard on a dog's body. During the surgery, she will be put under anaesthesia and she will need to stay at least one night so I can monitor her. After that, you will have to make sure she follows a strict diet until she heals. It should cost about..."

I began to feel faint. Not even including the x-rays, the total cost of the surgery was going to cost almost a whole month's worth of wages. I had only had my puppy for two weeks, and she was already proving to be more expensive than I had bargained for. I debated for a minute. *Can I afford this? Maybe I can just hope she passes it without damage. No, I already brought her here. I might as well go through with it.*

"Yes. Yes, it's fine," I said, hoping he wouldn't notice how shaken I was by the decision.

"Okay. I will perform the surgery tonight. You can pick her up tomorrow afternoon. We will call you if there are any complications."

"Thank you," I said, preparing to leave the patient room. I looked at Sue and wondered if it was going to be the last time I would see her. She watched me leave the room with a look that seemed full of fear. The tug on my heart caused my eyes to tear up, so I quickly turned around to avoid further eye contact with her and the vet. I blinked several times, trying to make the tears go away before reaching the front desk. The receptionist handed me the bill which felt like a blow to the chest. I reached into my purse, pulled out my card, and wondered how many more times I would have to do this for Sue.

I went home, worried equally about my puppy's well-being as well as the money pit she might become. Having her only two weeks, I could only imagine how much more expensive she would become over the course of her life. *Was I really ready for this financial responsibility?* I had thought I was, but now that I was faced with a hefty debt, I was beginning to doubt. I attempted to distract myself by cleaning up my apartment, but seeing her empty kennel made me realize how empty my home was without her.

I tried to go to sleep early but I tossed and turned for over an hour before drifting into a restless sleep. *I stood in front of the vet. He was explaining that there were unexpected complications, and Sue had died on the surgery table.* I woke up in tears. I repeatedly assured myself that it was a dream and the vet would have called if there had been any issues. Still unsure of reality, I triple checked my cell phone before I could relax. Once my heart stopped pounding and my tears were dry, I had a revelation.

Even though I had not owned Sue for very long, I loved her unconditionally. She had filled a void in my life that I had not completely realized was there. She was my loyal companion; she trusted me with her life and asked for little in return. I would do anything for her and would do my best to not let money come between us. I made a commitment to myself and to her that I would be more vigilant in monitoring her to make sure nothing like this ever happened again. With a lighter heart, I went back to sleep.

The next morning, I headed to the vet to reunite with my puppy. Sue was still groggy when I scooped her up, carefully avoiding her bandaged belly, and held her close. She relaxed in my arms and I knew that the love I felt for her was mutual.

Chat
By Brigette Furlonger

A chatroom shimmering dark
Until she types "hi"
He writes "hi there" back
A conversation starts
His words on the left
Hers on the right
A bubble throbs
Indicating new entries
That the other wrote
Single lines of phrases
Black on white shine bright
Pulling tenuous strings
Of each other's heart
Lines come faster
Some from the left
Others the right
Entwining fingers of words
To each other's delight
Binding them together
With stolen moments night after night
Days turn to weeks
Now it's been months
He starts to tease
She can't stop her flirt
It grows with ease
Even blossoms when he queries
The panties beneath her skirt
Safety within the miles
Of internet cable links
Until one of them says:
"It's time to meet
Don't you think?"

Love Is A Dream
By Dominique Megane Clinckemaille

Windows of the soul, an inferno
Her eyes, filled with fire
I feel her there
Feel her stare
Her features are a blur
The moon hiding behind the clouds
As if afraid of her

The girl from my dreams
Against the extraordinary she leans
Her movement is poetry
Every breath flowing through me
Her character is raw
Her spirit sours

She appears in this winter wonderland
Trees stand with pride so tall
Her heartbeat echoes through it all

She is spellbinding
Disappearing before my eyes
I'm left staring blankly
At the space where her shadow no longer lies
Her footprints in the snow
As there are stars in the sky

She remains unseen
But now a part of me
And through her eyes I see
Now all doubt set free
She really does love me.

The Birth Of Signs
By Alan Murphy

(After an essay on Miró by Jacques Dupin)

How does an ear of grain
turn into a kiss?

In a process of alternation,
alliteration and implosion
whereby the level table
on which it rests
is atomised,
its powder rouging
a new flat boundless space;
its stem abbreviates
to the smooth calculus
of union;
its kernels morph
into wayward murmurs;
and its tendrils become
the guttering flames
of love.

First published 2016, by Degenerate Literature

Fire and Desire
By Chris Kempling

A setting sun
Halos young lovers
Fire framing desire
Eyes closed, lips parted
Carrera marble throat
Stretching under
Strong cupped hands
A zephyr's breath
Teases a raven's wing
Of waist length hair
Sooty lashes brush
Rose tinted cheeks
Is there anything
More beautiful
In God's creation
Than just kissed lips
She tears away
But carries with her
The molten memory
Of being cherished
Her demure smile
An entire poem
Fire and desire

Hello, I'm In Eastleigh
By Marc Brightside

You looked like the real thing, bundled up
in shades of brown; we were the only ones
alive outside, un-drunk, un-hypnotised
by earphones or Facebook, and we laughed
together on the early-hours coach from Winchester
to Eastleigh – Beastleigh, Mrs Sark would call it.
Was it trust or confidence that held my hand
and led me to your home for awful tea at 2am?

Your name was Caroline (call me Carol, please,
a month sooner and it would have been hilarious),
ambiguously Asian with vanilla hair
and a slightly crooked smile. 'Why do you apologise
for eating in front of me?' I wish I'd asked.
'What brought you here from Plymouth?'
We woke your house-mate, but you didn't care
because apparently you never liked her anyway.

I'm not going to think about you
and I'm not going to call.
Ten minutes down or sixty miles off,
this doesn't change a thing.

Previously published, in *Litmus 2016* and *Vortex*.

Wild And Innocent
By Dayle Ashton

When I fell in love
For the first time
I was only eighteen years old,
With his faded jeans,
White cotton t-shirt,
The way he touched me
When we were alone at night,
Making out in the park,
Eyes sparkling in the street lights
Walking home in the early hours,
Holding hands tenderly,
Long kisses goodnight,
Promises of love everlasting
For two lonely hearts,
We hung together constantly
In those wild and innocent days,
Finding special places
For the two of us,
Where he kept me safe
From the darkness,
Taking me for the first time
As I surrendered to him
Beneath the peaceful stars
With romantic dreams
In my head,
While he played
A sweet serenade
Through the night
That left me singing.

Come Love Me Between The Sheets
By Courtney Speedy

Come love me between
the sheets and let our
bodies finally meet.
We're both a bit drunk
on vodka and love but
that's alright and it's okay
because I know you'll stay.
It took us four years to get
ourselves here with our
limbs loving each other.
Let me write poetry on
your beautiful body in
the dark as you run
your pale slender hands
through my hair
without a single care.
I will hold you close to
my scarred skin and
tell you to undress me
if you wish because I
want to feel your love
and your warmth against
my fragile bones and body.
How about just one kiss?
Ignore the scars on my
wrist and shoulder blade.
It's the bitter price I've
paid from an affair with
death and last summer
the devil offered me meth.
Time is running out
for me to be happy
so let's just be.
I'll curl up in the
curve of your arm
as your body moulds
into my frame.
Tell me this kind
of love is a gift
sent from above
and you'll heal my

god forsaken pain.
So come love me
between the sheets
and shout it out from
the sunny streets.
Love me in ways only
another poet could.

The Artist
By Angharad Thompson Rees

I laugh at what I once thought was love -
Tiny insignificant feelings,
like floating dust captured
by sunlight within the best room.
Pretty, yes,
but not in comparison to the
depths of the ocean, and
just like the hidden world
that lays in the deep blue,
you introduced me to an entire
new world. A world where
everything is gilded with crimson
and gold - secret feelings of passion
and hope.

Exquisite pleasures.

You took me from a world that was once
as if looking through a darkened
window, images outlined but no
depths.
No colour.
Ah! That is the greatest gift you give,
as if you paint a rainbow
on a blank canvas with your bare
hands as you caress my skin.

Like an Artist,
you expertly bring flowers
to life, and create colours that had never
existed,
compose songs within my heart that have
never been sung, and
place the moon within my palm.
Ah! You may say my poetry brings
joy to your heart, but your heart brings
joy to my poetry.
And what were once words
are now fragments of my soul.
And this, in return,
is my gift to you.

On The Bridge As Darkness Falls
By Clare Lightfoot

On the bridge as darkness falls
She leans across to watch the water,
And breathes in the heady
Scent of the evening flowers.
She waits.

On the bridge as darkness falls
She leans over into the water.
Her hair blowing in
The gentle breeze.
She waits.

On the bridge as darkness falls
She sighs and thinks of her love.
Tall, handsome, gentle.
Her sighs deepen.
She waits.

On the bridge as darkness falls
She hears the owl's eerie cry.
The horse whinnies softly.
She runs her hands through her hair.
She waits.

On the bridge as darkness falls
She sits on the bridge.
Eyes dreamily reflecting the water.
Thinking of her love.
She waits.

On the bridge as darkness falls
She drifts into sleep.
Dreaming of her lover.
To come and awaken her
with a kiss.
She sleeps.

On the bridge as darkness falls
She stirs, a sound! a voice!
Disturbs her slumber
Is it he?

She waits.

On the bridge as darkness falls
Her senses heighten!
Her breathing quickens!
She is afraid!
She waits.

On the bridge as darkness falls
She slips into the shadows.
Her breathing measured.
Her body still.
She waits.

On the bridge as darkness falls
She never sees the danger!
The blow is swift
And deadly
She breathes no more.

On the bridge as darkness falls
Her lover comes.
Her life has past.
The kiss they share
Lasts an eternity!

On the bridge as darkness falls.
Her lover departs
full of sorrow.
His love is gone
His heart is broken
He cries on the wind!

On the bridge as darkness falls
All is past but not forgotten.
Each night through
The years ahead
She waits.

On the bridge as darkness falls.
Each night
She awaits her lover.
She remembers
His kiss.
She smiles.

On the bridge as darkness falls.
The centuries pass.
The bridge remains.
New lovers come and go.
Their love immortal.
She remembers.

On the bridge as darkness falls.
Her lovers kiss
Blows on the wind.
To catch her
Unawares
She blushes.

On the bridge as darkness falls.
He takes her hand
Dries her tears
Kissing away her sorrow
His lips are warm
She remembers.

On the bridge as darkness falls.
A brightness
Descends upon them.
Catching them both
With laughter.
They smile.

On the bridge as darkness falls.
The lovers
Their souls reunited
Throughout the
Centuries of waiting
To wait no more.

Midnight
By Katie Lewington

tonight I am alone
and sleeping in my own bed
s'not the sex
but the company
the living with you.

Home
By Kirsty A. Niven

The sun ducks down behind the hill, glowing amber,
and we are left to our own devices.
This house we stand in, now our very own.
The backdrop for every future photo album,
every possible smile; our castle secured.

The cardboard towers around us crumble down,
allowing us some normality –
familiar things litter the place, marking our territory.
Chesterfields and tartan appear,
new mixing in with the old.

We sit in our fairy infested garden,
on this bench we built –
serenaded by sweet little birds
and sheltered by a wall of trees,
we see happy years roll out before us.

Forgiveness
By Elspeth Glenday

how do we come
to forgiveness

I always
loved you
he said

I saw the story
behind the words
and was no longer
lost

All The World's A War-Zone
By Nilanjana Bose

The flowers dry, the candles burn;
both reach their ends. The world still turns.
The streets are full, the café chat
is about revenge, tit for tat,
air-strikes, mortal wounds, ground combat.
I cannot take in any of that.
I only know she won't return.

Although each time the doorbell rings
my heart leaps once, instantly sings
then recalls the days before.
She'll never be back at my door.
The talk is thick with migrants; war;
how exactly to settle the score.
But I can't relate to those things.

There must be justice, and a stern
reprimand, offenders must learn
how strong we stand, crime never pays.
The news channels are choked for days
with some or other leader's speech-haze,
clips gone viral, constant replays,
rehashing the current concerns.

I just know that flowers dry rough,
that candles aren't warm enough.
I just know my room's gone cold,
my heart is shrivelled and grown old;
she'll never again cross this threshold
whatever events might unfold.
That's my truth, the rest's just stuff.

Let Go
By S'busiso Manqa

Let go
And I promise to catch
Not only you
But your feelings as well

Let go
Because I'm here to hold on
Hold you tight
In a manner of not letting go

Let go
While you keep your fears
With no doubt
I'm here to face them with you

Let go
With all this holding back
We're wasting time
And it's time to go on

So - Let go

Open Window
By Bernadette Perez

Wind soars pass the hour glass
Travellers criss-cross paths
Trampled by a brief period of time

Acquaintances that last a lifetime
While others drift apart
Some are never noticed

Emotions flourish clinging together
Helping hands grip affection
Bonding with compassion
Embedding to thy heart

Closed are the curtains
Shelter from the sun
With arms spread wide
I fling the drapes open

Precious devotion observed
Speaks of priceless whispers
Understanding and understood
Willing to catch you in mid flight

Friends value this journey
Travel beside you
Hold your hand along the way

Upon my windowsill
A view to ye bestowed
My soul floats within a breeze
Destined to reoccur
This my friend I found in You
Fluttering upon return

Evanescent
By Lonita Nugrahayu

Sweetheart,
your way of loving
rhythm well with the way sun is setting.
Both...
are passing out of the sight,
in a blink of an eye.
Both...
are fading away from the existence
so quickly.
Unfairly leaving the breathtaking emotion,
in a painful silence.
Letting me wonder,
if I would ever again,
seeing you...
if I would ever again,
indulging myself into the sunset.

For something that fades away quickly,
darkness is the answer.

Right after the sun sets,
dark sky awaits.
Right after your love has gone away,
sadness awaits.

This dark sky,
this sadness,
this darkness,
stays longer than your love.

Here Comes The Bride
By Barbara Hawthorn

so we said   we'd play at her wedding
something suitably light   Elgar, perhaps, Eidelweiss
Love is in the Air, for sure
drinks and nibbles on the lawn
                           so we thought
turns out   she meant the whole thing
Pom, pom de pom, Here comes the Bride
Mendelssohn's grand entry
  Wagnerian flourish in recession
the proper stuff   not in our repertoire
    such a scramble to find scores
last minute rehearsal
                         polish of a sort
bride-to-be hovering there   one of us after all
but not playing this time   obviously
we sent her to make us supper.

later   standing in the kitchen
nursing mugs of tea
one of us thought to say -
thinking of her youthful quickness
fast footing it up the stairs   almost late for every rehearsal
heavy instrument swinging from her shoulders -
you do know it's not a true march? Don't you?
don't tramp down the aisle   left-right
you'll be at the altar before the intro is done...
she had never been to a wedding
western style   this was to be
a wedding in two languages
across two cultures
so someone offered his arm
paraded her   step-close   step-close
                                mini-paced
progression
all of us humming   pom pom de pom-pom-pom-pom

on the day   she nailed it   absolutely
I stole a quick look at her on her father's arm
floating in serene beauty
lost my place in the music for a bar or two
no ... I'll tell the truth

a sudden sentimental tear filmed my eyes
two bars of blinking
before the music cleared

Sparkage
By Pamela Scott

It was love at first sight;
we glimpsed each other once,
the battle over, the war won
and the rest nothing but history.

We sparked right away
as people sometimes do,
something clicked between us
and we just knew somehow.

It was the way you looked at me;
deep, penetrating eyes all over my body,
like you understand everything
about me in that moment.

I never knew anyone
who looked at me like that.
You saw all my truths
with nothing kept hidden inside.

We told each other everything
in those few moments of time,
every secret opened wide
light shining in our darkness.

I've never felt so connected
to another living soul,
never trusted someone enough
to reveal my darkest truths.

You see it all, you see it everything.
I can be myself around you.
You know who I really am
and I don't have to pretend.

You and I have Sparkage;
two souls wandering the same path,
two lights shining in this dark
and two fireworks lighting the sky.

No Greater Love
By Rhyl Graham

Quietly sitting by the old gum, she watched him swim in the creek,
With her bright eyes and golden hair, he could see that she was meek,
Showing off as all lads do, she saw he was tall and thin,
His happy smile had won her heart, tho' he had coloured skin.

They often talked of her family, who came from over the sea,
He told her of his elders, how they roamed this land, wild and free,
And it was then, they knew, that their two worlds had collided,
Their vow to each other; was never to be divided.

Tho' life was often a struggle, love and hard work saw them through,
They taught their children goodness. How to be honest, kind and true,
A home of joy and laughter, in their life they did create,
He knew his children loved him; they always met him at the gate.

Suddenly from over the sea, there was trouble on our door,
Our country had to play its part; he signed up to join the war.
For six long years it took its toll on those who went to fight,
Each one came home a different man, and most don't sleep at night.

Now life for this young family had to take a different road,
To help him through his bad times, each now had to share the load,
When memories came flooding back, his actions were underhand,
"It's just the war, children," she'd say, to help them understand.

Trying to forget the horror, he found solace in a drink,
But there were times when it took over and pushed him to the brink,
He found the kitchen pantry was the safest place to hide,
As he gathered all his family and pushed them down inside.

"Heads down! In the bunker!" he'd yell as he closed the door,
They huddled there in fear as shots rang out through walls and floor,
Then only when all was calm, would they gently crawl back out,
And hold his shaking body as he came through another bout.

These times were part of life now, and she was always by his side,
He ignored all the help on offer, far too great was his pride.
The children grew to hate him for what he had put them through,
They chose to leave it all behind, but she stayed, forever true.

The years passed and their life went on, so changed from their first love,
And love it was that held her to him, till he was called above,
She lived a peaceful life now, no more times to be afraid,
The happy memories made her smile, but sad ones always stayed.

Her ageing years, they came so fast, she began to doubt her mind,
Some things she could see so clearly, even though she had gone blind,
Once again, she's by the creek, and she takes his outstretched hand,
"Come, my love, let's start afresh. There's no war in this here land."

Petals Linger
By Kathleen Boyle

Petals linger on cold, stone steps,
Bright against grey,
Soft upon granite
Fragile in the breeze.

Petals linger like our love
On the cold hardness of life,
too frail to endure,
but bright in the bleak.

Drifting gently over
granite planes,
petal soft love
lingered and was gone.

The Memory Of Desire
By Ronald L Kundinger

All through that long autumn
night I slept
fitfully yes, but sleeping still
and I dreamed
I dreamed of wet orange
and yellow leaves on the damp lawn
their pale underbellies
pointed upward at the moon
the air itself smelled of oceans
seas, salt and sweat, of us
pressed together in that sliver of moonlight
like cups, porcelain
filled to overflowing, compressed
to the breaking point, we shatter...
We are thighs and thighs
legs and feet entangled in the slick
night sheets, falling
like leaves into the morning
the damp dawn
till the sun burns it all
scorching the leaves to ash
and all that remains
as the smoke of the new day rises
is the memory
of desire.

Untitled
By Leon Stelmach

Why would I ever want to love again
As you in blessed sleep beside me lie,
What chance this faithful heart, already slain
To find the strength, the need again to try.
Loves youthful passion has with time abated
Replaced with something deeper and more true.
Love tempered and unity created
By each precious golden hour spent with you.
Your tender touch, a memory to treasure
I know you well and knowing love you, yet
The unknown revealed brings me only pleasure.
Through all the years there's naught to regret.
A loving cup, needs be with others shared
Love must not by complacency be impaired.

Murmuration
By Alan Murphy

An irregularity of the heart?
Lets listen; no, just a rumour.

Never Together Forever
By Kimmy Alan

No couple lives together forever
There is no such thing as living happily ever after
One of us will move on before the other
The other will be the lone survivor
So promise me this, my lover
Whose ever first to cross that immortal river
Let them wait with patient heart
To greet the other
When it's their turn to enter

My Father's Call
By Justin Fox

My father me phoned today
quite out of the blue,
his voice firm and true
down the crackling line.

As always he wanted to know
how my work was going,
how I was feeling,
what my short, medium,
long term plans were.

His voice was strong,
for strength is what Dad is,
a force in my life,
a compass, if you like,
that holds me to a course.

My father phoned me today
straight from the blue,
his voice so faint
down the long-distance line.

He apologised for not calling before,
things being different and all,
he apologised for not being there for me
as much as he would have liked,
and I said 'nonsense',
I felt him with me always.

My father phoned me today
and quite took my blues away,
for ten years ago he passed away,
and that long-distance call,
from who knows where,
will hold me true for another ten.

She
By Ryan Joel

I see her. Really see her. Not the colour of her hair. Not the fullness in her lips. I see her. Not the curve of her chin. And not the fullness in her bosom. I see her. I see her.

I see the gentleness in her spirit. I see it in her eyes. When she greets anyone. I see it. I see her. Brave and vulnerable. Yearning not wanting. Curious and sometimes brash. I see her. Playful and light. Yes. Yes. I see her.

I see her walk into a room. She's like a beacon upon stormy seas. They're drawn to her. Drawn to her light. Drawn to her innocence. She is like the Phoenix. Beautiful. Just. And unrelenting. They swoon and swagger. To be dismissed but with a smile. I see her.

I am helpless. Mesmerised by her essence. Drawn in like the rest. I must not succumb. I dare not give in. I cannot. I long to touch her.... mind... caress her.... soul. Bathe myself in her aura. Yes I see her.

I see her. Yet that is all I will ever do. I will see her. Admire her. Akin to the night sky. She shines brightest. And her laugh dances across the blackness in a flurry of light. I will marvel at her beauty forever. Simply because I see her. And she will never see me.

Fall For Me
By Courtney Speedy

Fall for me
and I promise
that I'll imprint
my poetry on
you forever.
Inky smudges
trailing down
your back and
running down
your broad shoulders.

2 Lovers Now Entwined
By Megan MacLeod

2 lovers now entwined
The perfect yin to the perfect yang
The perfect ebony to the perfect ivory
The perfect salt to the perfect pepper
The perfect bass to the perfect soprano

2 lovers now entwined
Joined together in wedded bliss
Hopes, dreams and future goals
Aligned forever with wonder to be hold

2 lovers now entwined
By a force of nature, life and love
Together they will stand the test of time

2 lovers now entwined
A perfect union
A perfect match
The perfect mate
The perfect start

2 lovers now entwined
A sweet embrace with lips and limbs
A surge and longing with lust and love
Go forward as one
Forever

Good Morning
By Carol Ann

I think of running my fingers through your hair;
massaging your forehead;
moving them gently across the temples.
I think of how they feel as I skim along your arms,
gently touching a sensitive spot.
Moving over your back,
softly prodding and massaging the muscles.

I can't explain how my fingers feel when I touch you,
but there is an energy in them.
They are sensitive to the slightest movement
and without me knowing why
they soothe and relax you.

And all the while I gently caress you,
I watch your face.
Watch for your eyes to open;
to see the colour, cool grey turning to warm green;
to see the love inside;
to whisper 'good morning'.

Previously self published in *Colour Me Alive*, 2011.

Solstice
By Jenna Rainey

Sun-drenched apparition within my drink-dazed view,
A long-sought after holiday spent alone with you.
Escape from un-reliant faces, distanced from public gaze,
No –one to judge or disapprove our joyful married haze.
Roaring fire heat of day turned down to warrant night,
Our blissful anchored paradise with passion set alight.
Too long withdrawn, cast miles apart,
Now united we heal the other's heart.

Spell suddenly broken as thoughts wearily drift,
To the real world left behind.
You reel me in to your all-encompassing arms,
Disregard any troubles on the line.
There's no worry that could burden me,
So long as you are mine.

Previously published in *Whim Magazine*: Issue 12.

Muse
By Joe Gallagher

Since I ever first saw her all I can do is think about her. The first time we spoke she told me something personal, a bereavement, her fiancée had been killed several years earlier and that day was the anniversary of his passing. I cried, she did too. I wanted to swap places with him but she shamed me by showing so much courage and determination. I went away and wrote a story, only for her, and returned the following week and gave it to her. She said she liked it and that inspired me.

I started writing more and more. Words seem to flow after I see her and speak with her. I will make any excuse to do so. I think about us being friends, enjoying each other's company. Maybe more. All I know is I admire her and want with all my person for her to be happy.

She is very beautiful both inside and out and, to me anyway, emanates a warmth and gentleness that is balanced by practical and emotional surety. Does she know what I feel? Does she feel it too? I don't know and I am too scared to ask.

Sometimes I stamp my feet in frustration at my cowardice, I want to tell her that I want to spend my time with her, my life with her, be friends with her, be lovers with her, but I hold back because I don't want to ruin the little that I have with her.

Sometimes I see her outside of her office but I never speak to her then, I am too shy and also don't want to embarrass her. She is young and beautiful, I am old and past my time.

I imagine a life with her, what it could be like, the love that could be involved, the things that we could share. She is helping me find a home, that is her position. I am without a home, that is mine. She wouldn't laugh in my face if she knew what I felt but I know she would never reciprocate, not to someone like me.

I ask God for guidance, I read Tarot for instruction, I ask the Stars for intervention, but nothing. With the little that I have I would rather have some of her time than none of her time, so I continue to visit her at the office, bring biscuits and talk about my housing. Try to tease more out of her but she won't give any more away.

The time will come when I no longer need her help and therefore will no longer see her. I am not looking forward to that. Do I love her? I am not sure, but what I do know is that since my first meeting with her my life has never been better and it saddens me that I can never thank her enough for what she has done for me or the impact she has made on me. Do I love her? It is the closest thing I have ever felt to the unconditional.

Love's Young Dream
By Frank Cardiff

When we go strolling, hand in hand
Some neighbours whisper "aint love grand!"
But we don't care if people know
Our world has such a rosy glow.

Tomorrow seems so far away;
The here and now is called Today.
Each hour has such a lot to give.
(When you're in love you love to live).

It's quite exciting "down the street"
You never know just who you'll meet.
We bill and coo just like a dove
And people say: "look, they're in love"

But surely there's enough to share –
There's always romance in the air,
A blossom or a tiny bud
A frog cavorting in the mud.

A sunset or a moonlit night,
A morning mist, an evening light,
A snowflake settling on a tree,
The quiet buzzing of a bee.

The gnarled old tree will give a wave
(With Apple Blossom After-Shave).
The Cowslips Moo, the Bluebells Ring,
We hear the songs the fairies sing.

My love and I walk hand in hand,
And if you're young, you'll understand
We're both still young and think it's great
(Well gosh, we're only eighty eight)

We have sweet memories of the past
And know just how to make them last
But if one day there's none to share,
A Guiding Hand will still be there.

Previously published in *The Accidental Poet* (ISBN 978-0-99411944-0-4)

Storms of the Heart
By Bee Parkinson

The thunder sweeps across the land
Swooping in through every crack on ground
Again the briefest flash of lightening
Electric blue so frightening.

The heat in the air begins to change
With some dark power a process starts
For particles themselves to rearrange
And the atoms within do tremble.

The body responds with hair raising
On back of neck and all patches of skin
With bated breath the world waits
For the eruption of the mightiest din.

In an explosion of proportions epic
The crashing and clashing of smashing and breaking
As all is turned upside and shaken till raw
By the ferocious and vicious side of nature.

Now commences the rain hammering down
The sound of the hooves of the apocalypse
Bringing tears to eyes and many a frown
As all wonder if they shall survive.

As the tempest rages onwards
The once cleared day turns to night
And in the darkness terror mounts
As tree's and posts soar high as a kite.

With one last wearisome groan
The howling abates and all is still
No longer does the sheltering house moan
As the rage and fury disappears.

Wreckage and debris are littered all over
Assorted objects strewn where they should not be
Temporary night slowly dispels
And the air is clear enough to see.

Such damage and destruction wrought

Upon those who feel they do not deserve
For their ropes of life already taught
No relief of reprieve for them.

The storms of nature cause destruction
On the physical level and above
Yet there are storms raging within us all
Mighty hurricane's borne from love.

The storm I witnessed that fateful day
Was foreshadowing the pain I was soon to know
For there is always a price to pay
For loving such a man as unfaithful as mine.

Cruelty
By Lonita Nugrahayu

We kiss our hello,
but we let our goodbye in silent.
We let go our first smiles,
but hold on our cries deeply within us.
We don't let the flower vase to break,
but we brake each others heart.

What is it in love,
that we tend to leave a scar because of it,
and let it be the tattoo,
in which the ink is invisible...
but the pain hurts deeper and doesn't go away.
What is it in love,
that we tend to have difficulty on being sober from its addiction.
What is it in love,
that the heartache of it,
is the future for so many of us...

We fall in love and later on, we rise in hate,
a hatred that we have for someone whom once we loved so much.
We are longing for love,
yet it is the fugitive that we want to catch, capture, punish, and later on execute it.

Isn't it a cruelty?

Could we love, and end it with love, too?
not with hatred,
not with silence,
not with brokenness.
Could the butterfly feeling of first love, first kiss, first touch,
last forever, until we no longer own our own breath?
Could the smile of first date be the smile of our everyday?
Could the words *I love you* stay?
Could we fall in love and rise in love, too?

Could we not relate love with cruelty?

Love Keeps No Record of Wrongs
By Lucy Reid

He drowned the offender's name in non-colour,
between the loaded bow of his writing hand.
For his ink could only bleed the pigment of his heart.

Sometimes or perhaps more often than mumbled
it stained decay wilt green.
Others like a bright bubbled surface scratch.

You could say the rarest of all
was the sea sickened blue.
For it lined everything.
And more importantly
it encircled this one name.

Every undirected anger,
bitten word, isolated decision
she had ever inflicted on her son's self or mind
was columned in his hand,
and her last words that morning were no different.

He had filled the pages of his heart with wrongs,
in so doing each piece added a next weight.
A weight that when carried too long would fall.

So it did.
The wrapped Book of Wrongs fell from his hands
one August afternoon when the heavens dashed the earth.
Little by little the book was warmed,
and its lines of colour ran from its prison
draining the spectrum of a rainbow.

Evanescence
By Andrew Hunter

Where does the time go
When your holding those
You love?

Time flows out of you
Into the love. And the love

Only grows
As your time

Goes

Love
By Madhumitha Murali

In the rustles of leaves
Making its own music
With the gushing air blows
On my face
That seemed to say something
As drops fell on me
The dancing fountain
With their light drizzles
The children's beautiful cries
As they enjoyed their game
At the park
All the beauty
That usually captured me
Seemed little with her presence
The world seemed concentrated
With the person I walked
Hand in Hand
Her voice was music
Her grace was charming
Her dancing earrings
Seemed to distract
Is this called love?
I dream...

Midnight Thoughts
By Heidi Al Khajah

There was a wall, indestructible
Some might say
No piercing that
But, your eyes and soul
They captured me
You wretched thief
You stole me right from under me
And my smile and your smile, are ours
Five minutes at a time
Like droplets in the rain
With our tongues held out
Trying to catch each one
In our game of life

A Friend For All Seasons
By Don Adams

The sunset strokes the gently lining face
and, through the window, silvers greying hair
as she prepares, in her accustomed place,
the evening meal, the two of us to share.

I sit and watch, immersed in reverie,
and dwell on days together, now and past.
The 'two of us to share', yes, that's the key
that promises contentment to the last.

We, both of us know this. No need for thought
or mulling over 'whys' or 'wheres' or 'hows'...
Throughout the years a growing love has brought
the knowledge that we've lived our marriage vows.

For true love comes not as a blinding flash.
This 'first sight' love can be a dangerous start:
It can so quickly turn from flames to ash.
No. Love at last sight proves the truer heart.

But, musing there, I sense a slight unease
as I look back upon the path we've trailed.
Perhaps my role gave me more liberties?
A wider scope while she was more curtailed?

As I set out upon my life's career,
and found success, fulfilment there at length,
a wife and mother kept the family near.
It's she who gave us love and gave me strength.

My patient partner, listening to my woes,
my selfish moans whenever times were tough.
For me it's been too easy to suppose
that what she had and did was full enough.

We both agreed upon our chosen course,
while one provides the other would support.
I don't know if there's ever been remorse
For chances other choices would have brought.

Was there a talent hidden, unexpressed?

A wider challenge that she could have met?
Was I too blind and selfish to have guessed
at other goals that she alone could set?

For no complaint has ever passed her lips.
Our home and family, these became her spheres.
Perhaps no other venture could eclipse
the labours, done for love, through all those years.

And now it's far too late to change our ways.
We are both set, whatever might have been.
But we are set in love throughout our days
and nothing on this earth will come between.

Sometimes I wish to write as Browning did;
to pen my love in lines that will not fade.
While in our time my fumbling tongue has hid
the tenderness I felt, but rare portrayed.

The twilight years have reached us all too fast,
our movements slowed and once straight figures bent.
But when I turn to look towards the past,
I see her near, and I am then content.

The day must come when death will make his play.
For one of us he'll cease his watching brief.
Oh let me be the one who leads the way!
Lest all around should shatter with my grief.

Season Of The Heart
By Frank Meintjies

she... spears dust on a pin of rain
weighs an eye on a cleft stick
erodes steel to its membranes
sips the slow night through a straw

he... shrouds the house in a tune
oils the lung of a carnival drum
throws rice in a cauldron
flicks a twinkle in the haystack

together... they slip a smile through the turret

Continue
By Katie Lewington

it's a cliché to say love is never giving up on the one that you love
but true
even when it feels easier to say fuck it, fuck off
I'm through with you
and to follow your head, telling you run
It's not
you are unable –

falling in love is special -
one time only deal
(maybe twice)
I don't want to be with a idiot, I wouldn't advise you to either but if he or she is
fun, feisty, loyal and makes your heart run laps
moody, snappy and occasionally grumpy but always right, eventually
and is the last to turn off the lights at night
then they're special, stick with that
everybody is human and has an array of emotions.

Malevolence In Love
By David Hollywood

As malice worships what he loves,
Your hearts pursued...! His wish thereof,
Will image scars that grieve to ache,
For velvet nightmares that awake,
From dreams which quest for all he'll take,
In rhythmic throbbings from your pulse,
Which consummates to fuse your lust,
With spite, that's bitten your impulse,
And found malevolence will thrust,
In search of longings that you've trust.

Lascivious are tortures charms,
When ecstasy in agony...! Rewards, enthrals,
Beguilings that shall drape your heart,
And penetrate desires delight,
When pleasure kissed you as his wife,
And venoms pain injects no life,
As visions that enrapture strife,
Are cravings for his passions bite,
Alluring you anaemic white,
To supplicate addictions fright.

And then your vampires relished heights?
Are mesmerized hypnotic nights.

The Air
By Lonita Nugrahayu

I wish,
you are the sun,
who comes in the morning and goes away right before dark.

I wish,
you are the moon,
who comes to lullaby the night,
along with the stars who show us how beautiful a darkness could be.

I wish,
you are the seasons,
spring, summer, autumn, winter,
who each comes to fill in our life with different flavours and colours.

I wish,
you are the rain,
who could be the mask of everyone,
so no one would know our sadness if we cry under the rain,
as it blends well with the magical raindrops.

I wish,
you are snowflakes,
the white beauty that drop from the sky just like pearls,
letting everyone to enjoy behind the windows, near a fireplace, with hot cocoa.

I sometimes wish,
you are a storm,
that would come once in a lifetime for a destruction,
a destruction that could strengthen the spirit within.

But my love,
you are none of them...
you are the air,
and without it,
there is no life.

My Universe
By Angharad Thompson Rees

Even now
your touch can send
stars falling from the sky
into my hands -
so I as hold you
I feel the Universe
in my palms.
And as if this gift
were not enough
your skin melts into mine
knocking me from orbit
with a Devine light
from the sight of your
eyes locked on mine.
I'll love you like the Universe
Forever, eternal and infinite.

Oswald
By Kev Milsom

Even on good days, the time difference between an uttered "goodbye" from my home-help, Mrs. Cooper, and the familiar double-click from my front door as she lets herself out into another Swansea evening, can take up to fifteen minutes. Tonight, I have a special reason for requiring her absence; namely the rusty, old tin that she has recently found at the back of a kitchen cupboard, clanking it down loudly upon the glass, coffee table before me. Her voice becomes deeper as she studies the artwork on top of the case, focusing on the trio of characters, stood leaning against a wall and smoking a certain brand of cigarettes, now long forgotten.

"My George likes those French ones...stinks the bloody house out, horrible things..."

With fixed, polite smile, I nod my head vaguely in the direction of her voice and issue appropriate grunts, just before receiving intricate descriptions of her husband's tobacco tin, along with some philosophical thoughts regarding pipe tobacco.

"Somehow it always reminds me of sailors... never trusted a sailor... something shifty about them sorts... bloody convicts, most of 'em.'"

As despair diminishes the corners of my fixed grin, I hear the fourteenth "goodbye" and the fifth "well I must be off" emanating from the hallway. Suddenly, like the former joyous sound of Christmas bells to my once-Christian ears, there falls a welcome double-click.

Across every day of the last four years, this evening moment of quiet has become a relaxing ritual for sinking back into my armchair, followed immediately by a serious case of lounging and pondering in the dark. Tonight however, post 'double-click', my arms are outstretched as I reach forwards for a once-familiar texture.

Eagerly, my excited fingertips run over the dusty, dented lid. A slight pull, followed by a 'twing' noise and I'm inside; each object splashing strong, single memories onto a mental canvas. Soft, folded edges of once-crisp cigarette cards releases childhood thoughts of Merthyr Tydfil in the '30s, where I spent notable Novembers with inseparable friends, Robin and Arthur, watching salmon leaping from the stream that ran through old Farmer Harris's lower field.

A gritty, steel pencil-sharpener yields mixed memories of St. Mark's; daily battles to avoid the swift, rapier cane of Mr. Jones, combined with genuine delight at learning of life beyond the valleys. Long-redundant, return train tickets to Cardiff initially signal a raucous smile upon my lips, screening scattered shades of a young man's idealistic dreams of the world and the endless sun-lit possibilities that lay before him.

Then, I think of her.

Instantaneously, my mind becomes a mass of shapeless shadows, blended against a slate, grey background, as if a beloved photograph becomes smudged beyond all recognition and blurs everything once precious.

In a fading fog-bound moment, my smile is gone.

At the bottom of my old tin, sheltered beneath a train ticket, probing fingers find the curiosity of a raised bump. A short search later, an object resting easily within my palm gives cause to sit in silent hope. The weight feels easy and right, as does the size and feel. While my index finger nostalgically traces the contours of the coin, a lone voice moves forward from 1972.

"We always said we'd buy something special for our Silver wedding. Well, this is both special and silver... if they can have a wedding anniversary present then so can we..."

Turning the coin over I reach for the centre. There, surrounded by raised filigree and a crown, I rediscover the letters 'E' and 'P'. I know this is it; a silver memento made in 1972 for her majesty Queen Elizabeth and loyal consort, Prince Philip, which long ago became 'our coin', minted especially for Edward and Pamela Harris from Fairview Terrace, Merthyr Tydfil, in celebration of their quarter century of wedded union.

Only when I find the dates marked upon the coin, '1947-1972', do the stout walls of my emotional defences finally yield; former, fogginess now swiftly replaced by dazzling sunbursts of simple, loving memories, dating back to 1946, when fate first welded us together within a Cardiff dance hall...*you, wrapped in a dress that shone with stars... me, a snotty youth in a cheap, demob suit, held spellbound by your blue eyes... summoning up battlefield bravery to approach you, just to hear what your voice sounded like...s o many hesitant steps before I finally stuttered words at you, like a broken machine gun... yet your smile simply grew in warmth and size...you took my outstretched hand... kind enough not to mention how much I was shaking... our very first foxtrot... my eyes locked upon yours as if blinking might cause you to disappear and leave my side. So many future days filled with light... climbing to the summit of countless summer hills to sit together and take in the beauty of the valleys beneath... hands held tight and the constant enjoyment of simply being in the warmth of each other's company... autumn nights laid upon an endless, grassy mattress, counting the stars and renaming the constellations for our amusement... how utterly beautiful you looked on our wedding day at St Stephen's, with the backdrop of countless sheep on the hills, like fluffy clouds against an emerald sky... everything you were and shall always mean to me...*

When the images finally disperse, all that remains is a clear picture of my wife, standing in the ancient, stone arch of St Stephen's Church; a veil covering her face. This is something so often imagined inside my head, yet this the atmosphere is different. This time, I watch her hands move upwards and remove the obstinate wedding veil.

And there she is; a radiant face wrapped in smiles... an image so cruelly denied me since her loss, seventeen years ago. Dark hair framing high cheekbones and eyes like dancing lights upon the sea – twinkling with mischief and wonder. Slowly, I take in every single line as the tiniest of details releases wave after wave of memories. As unfamiliar tears navigate my wrinkled facial features, evicting stubborn veils of grief, I lay my hands firmly upon my chest, catch my breath and lock your face to my memory forever.

Breathing heavily, my hand falls upon one final object within my tin. A present given on the first Christmas since my accident. A Braille version of my favourite book, *A Christmas Carol* by Charles Dickens. It still has the dent on the cover where I threw it angrily against the wall and shouted towards you. So many words on how I could never read it. How cruel you were to buy it. How much money was wasted on such a spiteful, futile task?

You never shouted at me. You simply picked it up and spoke gently into my ear with your lilting, Rhondda valley voice.

"Now then, Oswald. Let's try this again, shall we?"

The telephone makes me jump, stirring my guide dog, Lucy, from her peaceful slumbers. Instinctively, I reach across to my right and feel for the large button on the front of the telephone. Soon the lilting voice of our beautiful daughter is drifting around the room, increasing the volume of my smile.

"Hello darling, how are you? Yes Theresa, I'm fine... quite fine. I saw your mother today."

Birds of My Heart
By John R. Sabine

I see the lakeside birds in flight,
I see them rise in dawn's soft light.
They climb so swift on dew-heavy air,
Would that my heart could join them there.

For I hear them calling across the gorges,
To mates responding in a love that forges.
Where is my mate to share my call along,
A gorge of love to echo back my song?

The light's now bright and the birds have flown,
But my heart stays stuck on the ground alone,
For there is no strength that I can find,
To bring relief to my heart or mind.

And yet, and yet, the sun is in the air,
It flicks with flame the hilltops bare,
With light and warmth along the lake,
To grow and glow ... for my hearts sake?

And thus if my soul could only know,
That come one dawn a light would grow
Some other song for my heart to run
Some other love to catch the sun;
Are you ... that one?

Previously published 2012, O*n Thinking About It.* Ginninderra Press, Port Adelaide, Australia.

Lovely Motivation
By S'busiso Manqa

I want to see the world.
Roam the roads of ancient Rome,
Feel the warm clay of Mississippi,
And cruise along the aqua waters of Barbados.

I want to experience the afternoon
Traffic of Chicago,
Meanwhile I amuse my sight
With bright lights in Tokyo.

I want to be taught
Samba by a Brazilian,
Drink beer with a German,
And get a kiss on the Eiffel tower.

I just want to see
How the sun sets on a different sky,
Feel the winds breeze
On another man's land.

But all may not seem to amuse me,
Without you by side,
For only your love keeps me going.
So I say -

Keep your world,
If my ambition doesn't draw her towards me,
For this energy I possess -
Is just a mere conversion of my love for her.

The Trouble With Love
By Pamela Scott

Love's got no eyes
it cannot see
what it does to us.

Love's got no mind
it does not think
and acts without reason.

Love's got no head
it does not feel
or even care.

Love's got no brain
it cannot reason
and is irrational.

Love cannot feel
it has no heartbeat
and doesn't bleed.

Love's got no reason
it does not understand
or ask any questions.

Love asks no questions
it knows no better
and acts on impulse.

Love goes forth blindly
it sees nothing
and is unaware of everything.

Love's got no heart
it does not beat
or feel

Love's got no direction
it strikes out blindly
and too's and fro's.

What If All The Stars Went Out?
By Jenna Rainey

What if all the stars went out?
Would you run or stand to fight?
Attempt to build yourself a fortress?
Or cower from the black and endless night?

What if all the stars went out?
Would you seek to help your friends?
Protect your partner from the non-existent dawn?
Or turn the world's axis on its end?

What if all the stars went out
Would it see you at your best?
Turn kindred spirit, good natured-creature
Or revenge all those that you detest?

No matter if the stars go out
A secret can you keep?
I breached the edge because of you,
You're in now all too deep.

Warning Shot
By Michelle Lee

The day before Asteroid 2012 DA14 was scheduled to whiz past the Earth, Geoff Stern broke up with Libby Houseman.

"It's a warning shot," Geoff said, filling his backpack with his two Sociology textbooks, the jeans he never washed because he thought any bit of clean would ruin the fade, and the blue Colgate Firm-Bristle Libby had given him long ago when they had begun their run of overnighters, weekends, and the occasional Hump-Day eve (he always called Wednesday night that, then laughed like a boy). Libby didn't know how long Geoff had the jeans, but they'd been around longer than her. He had worn them the day they met two years earlier.

Geoff Stern and Libby Houseman been put in the same group in SOC100 and had to determine, along with two other classmates, what they would do if everyone else on the planet died and they were the only ones left. Libby said she would procreate with him to save the race. He was six-feet tall, weighed 205, and ran a mile in thirteen minutes, if he was promised a hoagie at the end.

Geoff had asked Libby out that night. They moved in together three months later.

"We have to heed it."

Libby tried to tell him it was going to be 17,000 miles away; no way could it even be considered a warning shot, a close call, a near miss. She tried to tell him there was no chance DA14 would hit the Earth and shatter it in a million pieces. But Geoff took the opportunity to quote Morgan Freeman, who played God more than once which, as Geoff insisted often and sometimes while he and Libby were in bed, was the reason Morgan became president in *Deep Impact*, even though Libby knew for a fact that role came earlier in his career than God.

"You have a choice. We have a choice. Right now."

Geoff usually said that with gusto at eight in the morning before leaving for his first class, hands on hips, facing the pantry and three boxes: his Cheerios, his Special K, and her granola with raisins. He always chose the granola. And he always picked out the raisins before adding soy milk and piled the wrinkled black bodies next to Libby's plate.

Libby replied the only way she knew how, in the language of the Freeman, of Him: "Cue the cheesy inspirational music – "

That was usually Geoff's line, after he made Libby work so hard for an orgasm that "I love you" tumbled out of her before she could stop it. But this time, he didn't smile, even though she still did.

He took her copy of *Wuthering Heights* and his copy of *Lord of the Flies* and stuffed them on top of a Green Day t-shirt.

"Did you know that in 1908, a slightly smaller asteroid exploded over Tunguska, Siberia, leveling trees over 2,000 square kilometres?"

Libby didn't reply. When his bag was full, Geoff dry-kissed her on the lips and went out the door, the only way in and out, of their small apartment. She watched him through the small window over the sink. He threw his backpack into the trunk of his dad's old Corolla, climbed into the driver's seat, and started off in the direction of survival: four miles down the road, two blocks past a Starbuck's and an HEB, in a subdivision called Sterling Oaks. His best friend's father lived there. Fifth house on the cul-de-sac. Two-story Texas rock, three-car garage, and an unfinished wine cellar. Cinder block walls.

Down there, underground, Geoff and his best friend-since-grade-school Chris would sleep on air mattresses, eat freeze-dried stew they bought at REI, watch *Firefly* on their laptops, and talk about existential bullshit until Geoff got tired of another man's swearing in his sleep and strange smells he never wanted to talk about at length. Until Geoff realized DA14 had passed by the Earth and left it just as it was.

Then, he would start off in the direction of survival (four miles up the road), park his car in the empty space, unload his backpack from the trunk of his dad's old Corolla, and walk back into the apartment through the same door, looking like some ragged disciple dismayed that God didn't choose him and muttering that it was good to be cautious about these things and one never knew what could happen.

Geoff would never say he missed Libby, though he'd let her choose some indie film for them to watch after Chinese food - the springrolls, the garlic eggplant – that she liked. He'd bury his nose in her hair for the entire two hours.

Three planetary threats so far.

Libby left the window and dragged a barstool (one of two tucked beneath the counter) over to the pantry. *It was good to be cautious about these things*, she thought, opening the door and finding the box of granola. She climbed the second rung of the stool, level with the top shelf, and pushed the box all the way to the back, behind the paper towels, thinking of how many raisin bodies she'd saved from certain destruction.

You, My Poetry
By Lonita Nugrahayu

I wake up and I am grateful,
that I get one more day to write you.
The fragrance of excitement the moment sunlight approaches my window and gently touches my skin,
reminding me of our rendezvous,
the one that has been going on since the day you left me.

I am still here, darling...
and I don't have a plan yet to leave you, to leave us...

We were something, my love...
our tale was not just a love story.
It was soul connection.
For once,
I believed that soulmate existed.

As I spill my first letter, your reminiscent start to pour in.
And I let them to mix with the tears of mine.
Together they flow, my love...
Inside these words, I have found my warmth,
the one that I have been stitching up letter by letter.

After I spill them, I often trace them...
to feel it again when my fingers used to trace you and yours traced mine.
Inside this ink,
I waltz, I jive, I cha cha cha, I slow dance,
with you.

You are here, my love...
we are here.
You are alive,
inside the ink that I spill the moment sun rises until it sets,
inside the poetry.
You are, m*y poetry*.

Luminous
By Keith Nunes

watching the fairy boats
lip the waves
contort candidly amid azures and mauves

sprinklings of stars glisten on the bay
you apply rubies to cheeks
silver and gold to wrists and ankles
you shimmer, astonish

we're rising above gardens
all touched by rain where
Jesus' champagne eyes
are bravura bookends for
verses of the poets

where the space between us
is charged,
where a kiss is a life's work
where minutes elongate and
callow youths are incandescent

here amid the lustre and brilliance
we meet
for the first time
can you feel it?

Mornings
By Brian Langley

She shares my life, she shares my bed
Each day I wake and see her there
Breathing softly, her golden hair
Beside me on the pillow spread.
She looks at me with words unsaid
And silently I say a prayer
Of hope, she always will be there
My sweet and lovely sleepyhead

Tis time to rise and face the day
I watch her as from sleep she stirs
And stretches in her sensual way
I get our breakfast, mine and hers
Just milk for her, same everyday.
She laps it up, then sits and purrs.

Previously published 2012 in *You Could Write a Poem About That*

Sorry
By Courtney Speedy

I use to think I knew what love was but that was before you. You made me doubt everything about myself. I always knew I didn't deserve you; the way you loved me so loyally but the way I pushed you away so delicately. I'm sorry I couldn't have loved you enough with whatever I defined as love and I'm sorry I lost myself when I was trying to find you. I'm sorry it's been another week since we've spoke and I'm sorry I hurt you. I am really sorry but you deserve better than who I am, what I am and what I need. They say war is painful but hurting somebody is even worse. The shrapnel left in your soul and the bloody wounds that never completely heal. I'm sorry for hurting you and I'm sorry I pushed you away when really you were all I wanted but probably not what I needed. But then again, what is it I need? Is it somebody to watch over me and make sure I don't dissolve into a puddle of tears and vodka on the bathroom floor? Or is it somebody to scream and shout at because the world is all going wrong and I need somebody to blame? I know I am not easy to be with and I never said it would a walk in the park but there are good days and then there are bad days. On the bad days, hold me tight and make me breakfast in bed and on the good days, make the most of it and do crazy things with me. I want to go hiking with you, go camping, go skinny dipping and to see the world on those beautiful good days. I want to be able to hold your hand and know that even if you don't understand; you care and that is more than enough. I don't know where this is going but then again I don't know where I'm going. All I know is I miss you. I think about what could have been a lot. Would you still be fascinated by the way I made the lamest jokes? Would you know I don't drink coffee but love hot chocolate? Would you know there's a birthmark on my stomach and there's a fire in my heart? Would you still love me regardless of my faults and flaws? I know I would still love you as much as I do now and maybe even the wall I built around myself would break down as I began to trust and treasure you more and more. I'm writing this for you on a cold day and my feet are cold but my heart is colder because I am afraid to love you, afraid to let you see that I am like broken glass. I will only cut and stain you. I will only hurt you because how are you meant to love somebody with all you have if you can't even love yourself? There's a mark on my soul and a great big hole in my heart because I know you've changed me, the way I was and the way I am now. I wish I wasn't so dramatic but I am just saying how I feel because otherwise I am scared I will forget this feeling and doubt it was even real one day. You would have left me sooner or later though, because the hysterical calls at midnight would have gotten tiring and let's face it; I can't stay in bed my whole life. You wouldn't have liked that. You wouldn't have understood and you would have gotten mad and you would have been so frustrated because you want to help but hey, what can you do? Nothing, that's what I would have told you. But you would have felt down then too because it isn't good enough and you can see something is wrong but you haven't known me for that long. I'm sorry for the mistakes I made and the ones I haven't made yet but know I will. I'm sorry I have such a guarded heart when really love should be limitless. I'm sorry I go for hours without thinking about you then the guilt sets in. I'm sorry for it all, alright? I am so fucking sorry, and if the sadness in my eyes and the madness in my heart doesn't prove that, then what the hell does? I said I was sorry at least a hundred times and then I began to rhyme all the time, using words that should only be used on you. You have something about you that I can't quite describe but you make me feel alive. Every Friday night that passes by and every couple I see together is going to break me more than your words could because why does everybody else get their own happy ending, but not me? I know it was my fault and I know I'm young but I also know I loved you and I thought that was maybe enough. I am still so hesitant about things because I know I am capable of breaking people and that scares me because you deserve to be whole and untainted. I have words to describe you with every letter of the alphabet but the last one stands out just a little bit more but maybe I am just not sure. I wonder what you are doing now, I wonder if you become a pilot one day because I know that's your dream and I wonder if you will ever forgive me for the hurt I caused. I know it all sounds insane and people will say I am being over dramatic, but isn't the world around us dramatic? It's what people thrive off though. Drama is what drives people and as sad as that is, it's 100% true. I have said it before and I will say it one last time; I am sorry. I am sorry from the bottom of my heart that my words pierced you like a dart. I am sorry I lost your trust and spoke with a mouthful of rust. I am so sorry and I know that the word itself doesn't do me any justice. But there is nothing else I can do because you wouldn't believe me, would you? I guess there is a healing period where it starts to get better and the words start to make sense and I can look at life in a different view but what's the point if I don't have you? So yeah, I am just going to keep loving you like I do and maybe one day you'll come back to me again and I can be forgiven for the pain. But until then, goodbye. I think it's time to let the birds out of their cage and let them fly. If you don't nurture something, it dies but I don't think that is the case with my feelings for you. Even if it wasn't for long, it was great and that's enough to know it is going to be tough. But sometimes enough is enough and I don't blame you for leaving but if love could have saved you, you would never have left.

Naked
By Pamela Scott

You make
me feel naked.

I become emotionally,
physically, mentally
stripped to the bone and raw.

My walls just disappear
when you look at me the way you do,
and make me feel so vulnerable.

I feel so naked around you,
my camouflage, barriers, walls
and layers of insecurity disintegrate.

My Love Hive
By Kariuki wa Nyamu

My love
in my heart you've found a permanent place
for when I look at your cheery face
shining like the new moon at night
My dear, tears of love drop in an impulse of delight
For sure, my love for you is more than words can say
an encouraging smile which I pray
that it'll last long enough to be enjoyed
and heavily consumed!

My love
When I look deep into your arresting eyes
like the stars in the skies
I become crazy with joy of having you near me
for you've stolen my heart, my love to be
For sure, this is the best ever made choice
for each new day I'll rejoice
and yearn to offer you anything there is to give
the best being my love-hive!

Once in a while
I see your mouth twist into an alluring smile
and wish that you'd fly to my arms
give me a long kiss that charms
For sure, my love for you is great, kind and right
Yes, I know that's what it meant to be, quite alright
Hoping to have no one else, remember
I'll love you always
so let our love be everlasting
at all our love's weather walkways!

Bolivia
By Kathleen Boyle

In love, on the mountain,
We watched the sinking sun
And the rising moon,
While pan pipes drifted
Through the dusty valley,
And we descended
To a rugged track
With startled villagers,
Remotely eking out a life
From dry Bolivian soil.
'De donde vienen?'
I heard a wizened wise one say.
Where have they come from?
From paradise,
I silently replied.

Ecliptic
By Rosie Mapplebeck

For Jaime

With love
we've carved out
your careful absence

In memory
a linear trace remains
our familial history

Meanwhile you etch
another arc with light
I cannot guess

Fitting then: your life
lit by sunrises, mine
warmed by sunsets.

Love's Malaise
By David Watt

Doctor can you tell me, is it love that ails me so?
You're trained in heart conditions and I have a right to know.
I seek a diagnosis, not a remedy or cure;
For if love's the explanation I will happily endure.

You may liken my affliction to preoccupied malaise,
With symptoms easing only under treatment of her gaze.
When I look upon her countenance my pulse begins to race,
And my heartbeat charts a rhythm tracing contours of her face.

I have no rash to offer, but my skin is prone to tingle
When she calls me ever sweetly or our bodies lightly mingle.
And her fragrance conjures magic, sets my senses all a quiver.
So be sure to check my temperature to validate my shiver.

My hearing may be failing – I miss much of what is said,
As if I'm in a tunnel and her voice the light ahead.
The melody my ears may hear allows her words alone
Irrespective of the distance, over barriers of stone.

And my appetite is changing – it's her nourishment I crave;
Tell me, is it serious? I promise to be brave.
I long for tempting starters, delicious tender mains,
Sweets of lip's creation, drinks pure as summer rains.

You say my ills are chronic – sure to linger through the years.
This reassures me greatly, truly solace to my ears!
For call me hypochondriac or words to that effect,
I prefer to live with love's malaise and treat it with respect.

30th September, 2013
By Kirsty A. Niven

An autumn day closing with a kiss, wine scented,
and you gazing up at me.
Fingers threaded together, entwined by glorious vows.
Made before the aging anvil, a token of history,
stated with quivering voices and sealed with tears.

The guests are heading home, driving country roads
and leaving us to silent bliss –
caressed by white linen and pillow clouds,
only the clink of the wine in the ice bucket.
"Wife," you murmur with a grin.

If there is a God, he must look down like a proud artist.
This moment, his finished masterpiece.

The Great Compatibility Quiz
By Jennifer Riggs

'Oh Darling, here's a quiz, do let's do it together. It's called To Wed, or Not to Wed – all about compatibility – see how well we'll get on together.'

'We don't need a quiz to tell us that.'

'Oh come on, it'll be fun.'

'Don't forget what's fun for you, may be death for the dog.'

'What dog? ... oh don't be silly, it's just a bit of fun. I love quizzes. It's not as if you're doing anything else ... ' He was doing something else, he was lounging with a post-coital smoke – part of the ritual as far as he was concerned.

'All right, then ...'

'OK. Part 1 – it's called – wait for it – Com*bed*ibility.'

'Expect me to laugh? What does it say?'

'Question 1 – Where is the G Spot?'

'Search me – part of a guitar?'

'This isn't about music – that comes later ... give up? I'll show you one day if you're good.'

'I am good.'

'So you say ... anyway, next one: 2, Which side of the bed do you prefer?'

'You know that: I sleep this side.'

'You do ... and that's where I sleep when you're not here – do you know, you've never once asked me?'

'I don't have to ask you, I go where I go.'

'Oh like that, is it? I go where I go – typical man.'

'Well, what do you want me to be? You wanted a man, didn't you?'

'Oh I was panting, was I? Let me tell you –'

'I'm tired of you telling me – get on with the quiz, if you must'.

'Oh well: 3 – Are you "early to bed and early to rise"?'

'You know damn well I'm not.'

'That's why I can never get rid of you.'

'Oh, want to get rid of me now?'

'Well, I'm early to rise, when I have the chance ...'

'Nobody's keeping you, get out!'

'This is my bed, you know. You get out!'

'I'll get out when I'm good and ready. I'm not one of the Wham, bang, thank you ma'am brigade!'

'Yes ... I hadn't noticed much in the way of thank you.'

'Huh!'

'OK – we'll be on safer ground here – This section's called Income-patibility – you have to see it written, look.'

'I'm not a complete nong, I can recognise a pun when I see it.'

'That's why I showed it to you.'

'I mean I can see a pun when I hear it ... never mind, go on.'

'First question: If you won a million dollars, would you: Quit work? Start up your own business? Keep on as you're going? Other? Want to know what I'd do?'

'Thought you were asking me.'

'We're both doing this thing, remember? OK what would you do?'

'Nothing. Invest it.'

'God, what a stick-in-the-mud! I'd get myself a whole new wardrobe and then travel.'

'Typical woman!'

'Seem to have heard that before ... well, isn't that what you were looking for? Would you prefer a freak? Or even a boy-friend?'

'Now we're seeing your mean streak – talk about drama!'

'I only said ...'

'That's your trouble, all mouth, typical woman, always too much to say, never know when to shut up.'

'You're so bloody-minded, I don't even want to ask you the next one.'

'Go on ...'

'Do you think all money should be shared in joint accounts?'

'No I don't – I'm not going to have you buying new wardrobes and haring off overseas every five minutes. What's mine's my own.'

'OK then, what's mine's mine. Two can play at that game.'

'We're getting on well, what's the next one?'

'It's about tax.'

'Groan ... A tax attack ... OK, shoot.'

'Do you believe you have a right and a duty to avoid tax by any legal means?'

'Certainly do.'

'Is that why you're marrying me?'

'I don't see you being very useful as a tax deduction. More of a liability ...'

'But what if I left work to have babies?'

'Who said anything about babies?'

'Well ... anyway they're tax deductions.'

'Expensive ones.'

'Well if Labour gets in, nappies will be GST free...'

'Not quite enough incentive for me - our leader's pro-family and pro private schools – we'll save a bit of money there.'

'That's really selfish stuff – I happen to believe Marx was right when he said "to each according to need, from each according to ability".'

'Oh, I've got a Red in my bed now!'

'I keep trying to tell you this is my bed.'

'Always got an answer ...'

'Well, this is a questionnaire, you know... Let's have your answer to this next section. This one's called Housemates. First question: Do you think a wife's proper place is barefoot, pregnant and in the kitchen?'

'I've no objection to you wearing shoes, I've been avoiding pregnancy on your behalf ever since I've known you and I'm more than happy with the deli round the corner. Answer your question?'

'Oh you ...'

'Come on, next question, I'm beginning to enjoy this.'

'Contentious bastard!'

'What would be your priority: Lock-up parking? A good-sized spare bedroom? An ocean view?'

'Are you joking? Who wants to park a Ferrari in the street?'

'You haven't got a Ferrari.

'Not yet, girl, not yet. But if you keep out of my hair long enough I will. Babies indeed! No sense of priorities! No vision! Typical woman.'

'You're getting f... boring. I don't like what I'm hearing. No. Not one bit.'

'You're not the only one ...'

'Next question: Do you ever leave the top off the toothpaste tube?'

They looked at one another in horror, hardly daring to speak, and then spoke as one. 'No! Never!'

They collapsed into each other's arms, laughing joyously. They had achieved true compatibility. The future stretched before them, beckoning, rosy. The post-coital cigarette had actually been an inter-course cigarette.

Love's Not A Christmas Thing
By Nilanjana Bose

I'll love you with the dance in my bones,
and the pigeon calls in my veins;
with the soil of my flesh and its stones,
the bungled belly laugh in my brains.

I'll love you when the dances get dim
when the anklets grow hooks and draw blood;
when pirouette is brimstone and grim,
the last thrash of fish on the mud.

I'll love you when the tinsel's trash
when the tree's just needles on the floor -
all festive is only one flash,
and dark is the maw of the door.

I'll love you still when the music thins
under the amber songs of dawnskins.

Calypso's Lament
By Helen Bowers

Not the first girl to fall for a sailor
won't be the last but ah! the bitter
sweet savour of salt on his lips
and the lilt of his voice as he sings
of the star-studded sky and the wine dark sea,
of battles lost and won and ah!
the hunger that burns in his belly
and bones for a woman's yielding flesh.

Any woman would do but he tells you
there's something about the cut of your jib
that he's dreamed of ... longed for ... found.
So you drown full four fathoms deep
in his sea-green, seafaring eyes and you feed him,
warm his bed against the chill that moans
in his dreams, urging him on and on.

He slips through your fingers a strand
at a time drawn due east beyond you
and the child at your breast to the old ways,
the old lays that contour the lie of his land.
One grey-fingered dawn and he's gone,
no mention of postcards or child support,
not even a backward glance
at the flotsam he's left in his wake.

Soul Song
By Ryan Joel

I have known you before a time of knowing. Before my body took form. I knew you. Before each cell had started becoming it's purpose. My soul had glanced at yours. That was all it took.

I have known you for an eternal lifetime. But I have never met you. I've known your fears. I've seen your spirit. The colour of your laugh. Has comforted me when my world was grey and dreary. The scent of your smile has calmed me through times of angst.

Through time you lived within me. Safe. Flawed. Imperfect. Beautiful beyond compare. That is where I came to know you. We spoke words unseen. In language unknown. We sang our soul songs. Harsh
Brittle. Soothing. Moving.

Others sneered at me. And in time. I too believed that I was mad. Tainted. Sad. For believing. For yearning. Yearning for you. Your smell. The embrace of your presence. The touch of your essence. Just you. I began to lose hope. I faltered. I lost my way.

And for this I am sorry. Sorry that I gave up on you. Sorry that I became disconnected. Sorry that I never kept believing. And the last spark of you. I kept safe. Hidden. Protected. And that would be what I had. If at all anything. For as much as I stopped searching. The yearning grew stronger. And at times it felt like I would burst.

At the precipice of my resolve. I set you free. I let you go. I saw you dance across the mountains in my mind. I saw you welcome the dawn with a kiss. And lift the sunset with your gentle touch. You were more beautiful now than even I could have envisioned. And suddenly I understood. It all made sense. This was your destiny. Your seeds were meant to be sowed. The splendour of which is surreal to behold.

And now. Now you're here. Here before me. How? When? Really? And every thought about how it would be and what I would say. Just that. Thoughts. Instances. I'm breathless. I'm ashamed. Ill deserving of your beauty. Your pureness of heart. Just one moment with you. Just a touch. Would be an eternity of bliss. I'll take it.

That one touch. Millions of galaxies imploding at once. A plethora of light and colour. Colour felt and not seen. And you are the catalyst. You are the fuel to my spark. And together. We'll bathe the universe in splendour. Because as sure as you Sow your seeds Seed Sower. I will till the ground beneath you. And the fruits of our labour will grow. And flourish. And the world will be a little better. Albeit within ourselves. This is my soul song. Thank you for waiting for me.

My Popsicle Toes
By Clement Clark

Only my aching heart knows
That once I met a rose,
Whose love was my daily dose
Cos she loved me the way love goes,
We accepted life anyway the wind blows
Forever in love and ever so close,
She'd tease that I'm her primrose
And I would whisper she's my popsicle toes,
Love did from our hearts flow
That certainly raised eyebrows,
For fun we'd frequent stores
At night shop through windows,
O, her eyes with glows
That touched my heart like blows,
At times she would humble those
Who prided themselves like flamingoes,
Yet only my heart knows
That just before I could propose,
She teased that I'm her primrose
Then died with both eyes close.

Pink Ladies Gossiping
By Keith Nunes

pink ladies gossiping in the back row
of a black and white movie
blue boys spray-painting a red
car green in a dirt brown yard

lilacs flower under a bronze sun
as red-headed Ruby raises an
ivory white hand to a man in a
yellow shirt who says: "I know you"

they kiss under a mauve neon sign
and drive away in his azure sedan
at his ochre-coloured house they
lie down on crimson satin sheets

Love Alive
By Dayle Ashton

It's knowing you'll be waiting
To meet me with a kiss,
Falling into your arms and
Pressing my body close,
Sighing with contentment
At being together again,
Sharing a glass of wine,
Believing that your shining eyes
Reflect the feelings in your heart,
Soothed by the tones of your voice
Leading me to your room
With soft circling caresses
Lighting the flame,
Growing more urgent
With the need
To be fulfilled,
Crying out your name
As we fall over the abyss
Together once more,
Clinging to each other
With words that have no sound
Before subsiding gently
Onto the pillow
Of sweet dreams
That keep our love alive.

Waiting
By Ronald L Kundinger

I have written you letters
In sweat on skin dry parchment
Telling you of spring here
And how the world and my words
Move ponderously down the same dusty roads
How the new buds breaking the earth
Remind me of your lips and eyes and rain
And how they all can soothe and cool like a soft tongue
How I sit here in my old robe of heat and longing
As my letters pile up at my feet like leaves
Ready to ignite at my touch
And I wait with fingers dry as matches
I wait for you to answer

Schnorthog And Schweethog
By James Scalise

Schnorthog's a warthog with shovel-shaped face
Baring a dreadful pout.
With four awesome warts and tusks like a razor,
curving straight up from his schnout.
A pugnacious nature and scary a creature,
As nasty a beastie could be.

His schweetheart, Schweethog,
has two hairy warts
on a face as fearsome as he.
He thinks she's pretty,
she loves his schnout.
Now isn't that all that matters or counts?

When they're together
Their love is so true,
They don't mind their warts or their smell.
Pieu! Pew! Pieu!
But don't all the warthogs also need love,
just like me and like you?

Now when they're apart they're oh so so lonely,
as lonely as lonely can be.
They so miss each other,
their smells and their warts
that it is just too plain to see:
They aren't so different from you or from me.

But they're not very fond
of us weird looking beings,
strangers like us whose oddness reviles.
We critters without curvy tusks or fine warts,
with such ugly faces, with no long tails,
we creatures whose strange smell offends.

So if you should ever
come close to their burrow,
it's not smart to stop and say "Hi".
It's better to back up
in a big hurry,
pass quickly by and just say "Goodbye".

Say It
By Guy Morris

It's not often heard, in modern day life.
Between Boyfriend, Girlfriend, Husband and Wife.
We get too complacent, always in a hurry.
We often forget, but seem not to worry.
Say it, to your loved ones, for those whom you care.
Before its too late and they're no longer there.
Say it, and mean it, to all whom you love.
And may God smile upon you, from heaven above.
Say it, right now, and bear no regret.
It may be the last chance that you ever get!
Of what, am I speaking? Why? Have you no clue?
It's those three little words, that say... *I love you!*

Met On The Net
By Barbara Hawthorn

love can strike out of the blue
a giddy gust to spin the senses
no anchors to fix the time and place
does the road to love really need
a quarried stone base?
must there be hooks to hang love upon?
that park bench   that summer cruise
the corner table in that coffee shop
bicycle built for two
lovers' lane   off memory lane
but where are the signposts on the map?
does that stairway to heaven have rise and tread
that submits to measurement?
 whirlwind romance   or virtual twister?

so where then did you meet
your little bright-eyed doll?
down by the riverside?
                or on some well chaperoned dance floor?
bible-class picnic to Potters Park?
or lock eyes with a stranger
 across a crowded room
some enchanted evening long ago?
what tulips have you two tiptoed through?
where plucked he that red red rose
that he pinned in your hair?

bluebells gathered in the merry month of May?
or lilacs in the spring
can you truly swoon over virtual fragrance?
was it April in Paris?   or did you shyly woo
your K-k-katie by the k-k-kitchen door?
on what tide-swept beach did you trace
those love letters in the sand?
sailing away on Moonlight bay
yes – memories are made of this
foolish things making moments to remember

love strikes out of a clear blue sky like I said
but cyber space is a colourless void

no rainbow sites on the worldwide web
technology groping in a murky cloud
in the shade of the old Apple tree
(we're talking Steve Job's sapling here)
greyheads wag their chins and suck their teeth
that screen, bright-lit rectangle, may prove
no magic casement
is it safe or sensible or wise?
                                    and yet... they met on the net

Sustain
By Andrew Hunter

After it

I was phoning you
by the bridge

and you were doing that thing
you do

So there's me
holding back And you
gone silent The birds

were screaming by the river
fighting for the bread
the old woman was launching

They crashed into the water
nipped each others' wings
The bread

soon disappeared
If it wasn't eaten by the ducks
it sank But

her wee arm kept spraying it out
I guess

she was doing
her best

Beloved
By Frank Meintjies

my beloved
stirs in the small ripples of the sheet
she is a face
without movement
calm as a coastal green field
my beloved
is as peaceful
as mid- December month
her spirit a holiday book
being read
the sun on a lock of her hair
brings stars into the room
her voice
a slight breeze blowing
cooling the day
I kiss her
and think of eating watermelon
in the shade
my lovemaking is naïve
simple/visceral/in the moment;
fierceness and fire
throughout the year
but now I revel
in your sweet spot

Loving You
By Akwu Sunday Victor

For Ene

It was that part of the year
When the egrets accompany cattle across
The luscious meadow

My love is the egret that does not bring forth blue offspring

Then, the sun
That monster of the sky
Glared upon the world furiously

My love is the egret that does not bring forth blue offspring

Forlornly my imagination
Like a goat in a tither
Orbited around without course

My love is the egret that does not bring forth blue offspring

And then the breeze
That unseen emissary
Brought into my nostrils your perfumed hair

My love is the egret that does not bring forth blue offspring

And there you stand
Like a spirit from the stream
Eyes bright as diamonds on a fleeting river

My love is the egret that does not bring forth blue offspring

My love for you is the egret
White as the sun's filament
Flowing, a lucid fountain

My love is the egret that does not bring forth blue offspring

There you stand, lips parted
Teeth sparkling

Your love is molten gold, taking shape in a mould of sand

The Day We Sang Love
By S'busiso Manqa

I fell in love
With a singer during rehearsal

It had nothing to do
With her rhythmic frequencies,
But something within her
That awakened something
In me

She awakened her abilities
Through the comfort of my words,
And I found inner peace
Due to her presence around me

I've known her
Since before her abilities
And she adored me
Before the discovery of my capabilities

See a while ago
I discovered the light in her eyes,
The might in her spirit
And the amazing effect she has on me

This is a case
Where the experiences of friendship
Lay birth
To what stops us from being more

If we're really made in pairs
No doubt comes to mind
When I fearlessly state
That this golden lady is my other half indeed

So golden lady I plead,
"Sing me a song
With all your might -
A song written by my very own emotions

As fear blocks us
From being more,

I plead for us not to stay as friends
Thou' I promise not to push for more

I can't pledge
Not to fall deep enough,
All beg, is for you not to repel -
As this feeling is arising to complete me"

My Love - For Wine!
By David Hollywood

This vine I toast, before my view,
It only flows for you,
And while I sip,
A touch so close to me,
I feel the ruby red, your lip,
My over flow, I see,
Encloses thoughts of only who,
This grace,
I taste,
Is all a sense of you.

I'm Standing At The Cross
By Courtney Speedy

I'm standing at the cross
waiting for God to come
and rescue me from my
mistakes and bitter fate
because it's about time
I opened my eyes and
realised that above me
are beautiful blue skies
and I am too young to
stay in bed and cry.
I want to be in your
sweetness and soul,
to feel blissfully whole
because you have me
tight in your grip making
sure that I don't slip.
The curve of your arm
around my waist assures
me that time spent with
you is never a waste.
I want to get lost with
you and run through
the streets hearing my
heart beat because this
is life and how it should
be lived because the next
day isn't always a given.
So tonight when the
sun sets I hope it will
be your hand resting
on my shoulder as the
weather gets colder.
There are stars in the
sky and weeks have
gone by but I shall not
weep and cry because
one day you'll get lost
inside my mind and
everything will be fine.
So tonight and the next
hundred years to come,

would you do me the
honour of keeping me
safe in the dark times
and hold me when all
I can do is rhyme?
Plant kisses on my
forehead and warm
my soul as you hold
me under the stars
at the cross in front
of God because this
is the life I've made.
So tonight will you
follow me down the
wooden steps to the
beach and help me
heal and reach for the
stars and the moon?
I wish I had found you
sooner hidden amongst
the night sky as the
waves hummed and
the birds sung from
the trees because I
wanted the curve of
your arm around
my waist assuring
me that I would be
fine but you came
by soon after when
there was not a single
cloud in the sky.

Time Lapse
By Helen Bowers

Last summer we lazed
on the sun-dappled veranda,
one long languorous late afternoon
after another, languidly nibbling figs,
iced melon and slivers of prosciutto,
winding down, loosening up,
with one glass of chilled Chardonnay
after another until, drunken sailors
on the rampage, we stumbled into bed
to satisfy a more ravenous hunger,
to quench a more urgent thirst.

This summer I eat take-away dinners,
feed cat, water pot-plants, watch news,
current affairs and an episode
of a mini-series of minimal merit,
ring two friends, neither one at home,
write shopping list, do some ironing,
drink coffee, brush teeth, have shower,
find that my laugh lines have deepened
into wrinkles, read another chapter
of the dullest novel ever published,
turn off the bedside light and pray
that daylight will blot out memories
of last summer … and you.

The Moment Of Passion's Fading
By Barbara Hawthorn

when passion fades
you may not　　　　at first　　　notice
like the relentless shortening of days
that sets in after the summer solstice
the gradual cooling　　of an embrace
curtailment of caresses that once
stroked a finger from cheek to chin
you may not notice
the moment of passion's fading

routine　　　will sweep you on
little niceties will be observed
devotion is a habit deep ingrained
our generation has such fine manners
socially trained to perform well
a long-running Broadway play
when does the cold truth dawn
that this is fiction?　　but then again
you may not notice
that moment of passion's fading

which is worse I wonder?
when passion goes　　if one knows
and the other seemingly does not
or if both chillingly know it's gone
but carry on　　neither relishing the role
of spelling it out　　chapter and verse
or if everyone knows　　　so pronounced the drift
yet locked in a scripted courtly dance
they never even notice
completely missed
that moment of passion's fading

New York Number One
By Kathleen Boyle

We met on East 55th with 7.
It was love at first sight
As we lingered over
Fresh delhi fruit whizz.

On 42 with 6 we stopped
For coffee and bagel
And New York buzzed
Around our bubble.

I got to know you better
As we strolled 6 with 10
11 and 12.
Your smile beguiled.

Time melted as our
Love blossomed on
Washington Square Park
And we kissed on 10th with 5.

Later, the Times Square neons
Joined the stars to celebrate
Our love as, hand in hand,
We glowed on 42nd with 7.

That night I lay awake
In my hotel, restless for your
Presence and longing for
The morn. when we would meet

On 2nd with 14th Street.
Or was it 7th with 14th?
Or 3rd with 22nd?
Or 9th with 42nd?

I never was much good with numbers.

This Thing Inside Me
By S'busiso Manqa

What is this i feel
Thumping and pumping
With such great might
Beneath my young chest

It seems quite stronger than my heart
Or is it my heart?
But this thing
Manages to control my every move

It has pierced
Through my daily innocent thoughts
Flashing to me
A constant picture of two

I have been warned about it -
I'm not sure by whom
Or what they said
But I remember the talk concerned this

This thing seems so powerful
It destroys – builds - inspires
You name it...
Perhaps I shall ask *love* about it.

Newborn
By Kirsty A. Niven

Oh little pearls –

Pink rosebuds, silken –
a fist, milky sweet,

Your tight grasp
clenches and releases –

Meaningful, needing.
Love washes over,

Love consumes
as tiny crescent moons

Pattern my skin –
tireless tattoos.

A wave of it
crashes against me –

Pulling me under,
gasping for air.

An emptiness overflowing,
a wound salted.

Such a little thing,
I can't look away –

A grip on reality,
both wrinkled and new.

The Pyramid Of Me
By Kimmy Alan

Despite the trappings of morality
At the bottom of every mortal's soul
Lies the bricks of our basic needs
Thirst, hunger, air, shelter, libido
Drinking, eating, breathing, breeding
But overlooked by Abraham Maslow
Every one of these basic needs
I need you to satisfy with me
For you are my Juliette
And I'm your Romeo

The Last Dance
By Chris Kempling

He was so glad she said yes
when he asked her to the prom
He'd been admiring her for months
an unattached beauty
She'd been too busy for boys
but something about him
the shy awkward way he asked
with a crimson blush
spreading up his sturdy neck
made her say yes
But not right away
because it was precious
to watch the unmasked eagerness
in his eyes.

She was a vision in green satin
the perfect match for her long
auburn hair, cascading in waves
across bared white shoulders
An orchid corsage, petals delicate
adorned a slender wrist
His jaw dropped as she descended
the curving stair
Desire mixed with awe clouded his words
All he could manage
was a low, *Wow*.

She stood on the first step
looking at his broad shoulders
made wider by the padded tux
His bronzed neck rose from a
white, gold studded shirt
A hand-tied bow tie nestled
at the base of his throat
while carnation and baby's breath
graced a black lapel
Under dark lashes she glanced
at the curve of his strong chin
as he helped her down the last step.

Her mother fussed and gushed
as her father, camera flashing, said,
Just one more shot
Their hands brushed lightly
on the way to the car
He'd forgotten to offer his arm
and practically ran to get the door
as his mother's admonitions
rang in his ears
Their eyes met as he held the door
Something electric arced between them.

As they were announced
everyone said, What a fine couple
Both were too nervous, and just
concentrated on not tripping
But then the first dance started
he with his mother, she with daddy
Everyone was waiting
for the traditional dance to end
After more pictures and tears
the parents drifted off
full of mixed emotions.

The night went by too fast
Sometimes they danced or
reminisced with friends
Sometimes they sat by the glow
of red-jarred candlelight
and talked of their plans
She was off to the big city
for an engineering degree
he to a Michigan college
on a hockey scholarship
My god - Michigan, he said
Then came the call
for the last dance

The music started softly
As the tenor's mellifluous voice
started to soar
they knew it could be the last time
they held one another
She laid her head against his chest

then lifted her face to press
her nose into the hollow of his neck
He inhaled sweet perfume
rose petals and jasmine
from her scented hair
and pressed her close
to feel her soft breasts
against his ribs.

Slowly they moved
without saying a word
eyes closed, as the bass notes
reverberated through their bodies
Why had they waited so long
to let their hearts intertwine
He stopped holding her hand
and put both his arms around her,
hands caressing a naked back
She linked fingers around his neck
and touched his ear lobe
with slightly parted lips
not knowing why, but only
that she wanted to.

As the last notes faded
they stood still
not wanting the moment to end
She looked up
first at his eyes
then at his mouth, wondering
hoping that he would
He put a finger under her chin
and kissed
first her cheeks, warm, soft
then lips, moist with passion
And when they opened their eyes
they knew
it would not be
their last dance.

Change
By Katie Lewington

my favourite place was
the library
childhood spent
head buried
within pages
far from reality
and now
my favourite place
is you -
drink food love comfort money strength motivation inspiration -
it all comes from you
willingly
love
love
love
pouring
as if juice from a beaker
into a mug

Blueberry
By Clement Clark

'Twas all through the love of cherry
That I met a girl called Berry,
She was a beauty from a place named Blackberry
Where she stood out like a strawberry,
Lovely-lovely, what a guava
My heartbeat was pickle and banana,
And when she smiled I saw peaches
I looked again and saw leeches,
Could I have gone off my millies
For I told her that I loved her more than chili's,
"Love is lovely," said my Berry
'Twas at the corner of Blueberry,
The mood was grapes and avocado
And the feeling was sweet potato,
She then lifted her dress shaped like an apple
And showed me her pineapple,
Bravely I lashed out my cucumber
O, lovely-lovely, what a guava,
Her moods were soon lime mixed with lemon
Her stomach looked like a watermelon,
Nine months later she got a child bluer than Berry
I named the child Blueberry.

A Touch Above
By Keith Nunes

You touch her through the cotton kaftan and she turns and anoints you with deliciousness and respite and sunshine so giving your heart disease leaves town, you knew it would be like this but you resisted - strung out on faux hanging offences and vaudevillian silliness, the lessons aren't engraved onto the inside of your skull so you don't remember them, you wonder: "should I be storing this sort of thing in the cloud?"

Those Rad Friends
By Molly Donald

I once asked for a piece of light -
something of clarity, to make everything feel
possibly all right.
But I was gifted with a sunshine instead; an awakening from all the dread.
The horrors on the news, consuming darkness believed to be true:
I found you.

People do not last forever - our heartbeats do not beat together,
we will not last together for our special forever.
One of us will leave, one of us will stay, for hearts drum
to different beats. And ours is not written on any musical sheets.
It is unknown and unplanned. There is no master plan.
Just people with hearts.
No matter how broken they are. One part may break, but the other will fill the space.

We are a peculiar arrangement.
Twisted harmony among the beats, we are a noise that others could not foresee.
A collection of unpredictable, hopeless, dreaming pieces.

A Settled Sonnet
By Kirsty A. Niven

I do not love you as if you are a sparkling diamond
or the roses of poems that can only be revered.
I love you the way real things must be loved,
out loud, screaming and laughing like a child.

I love you like every minute is ticking away
and the clock may stop and screech in alarm.
Thanks to your love I value every second
like a tiny pearl in the palm of my hand.

I love you and know how, when, where, and why.
I love you without envy, greed or violence;
I love you happily and peacefully as I should.

There's no use wasting a world where we both exist
on darkness and fearing the steal in the night,
when you are so close I feel your breath on my lips.

You, Me... Us
By S'busiso Manqa

The Sun
The Moon
Day,
Night,
Light And Dark

Two Opposites
A Pair
Me And You
We And Us

I Do All For You
As You Do All For Me
Hell Today
Our Heaven Tomorrow

Us – Naked
One Plus One
Equal To One...
Such A Lovely Formula

Hands Holding
Hearts Beating
Dreams Living
The World Was Built For Two.

The Dancers
By Barbara Hawthorn

they dance - not often
but I love to see them
watching him twinkling and twisting
flitting like a hummingbird
from wallflower to wallflower
around the dusty hall
- real live men are rare creatures
at these senior citizen dances -
it would be easy to believe
they come just for him
while she looks on from the sideline
overflowing the spindly church-hall chair
placid as a cow
ballooning bosoms pillowed almost in her lap
hands like hams planted on each knee
she nods and sings along
jowls and chins a-jiggle.

but then we play something
that might be called "their song"
something from a sweet past
and he toe-taps his way over
clicking his fingers and holding out his hand
such a surprise when she rises
to note the still slim ankles
who would have thought someone
so bulky would be so light on her feet
so majestically grazioso
smooth counterpoint to his toe-tapping syncopation
true he can hardly be said to lead the dance
she has been known to twirl him and dip him
holding him poised a beat or two
in massive arms

I love to watch her sail serenely
in the counter clockwise swirl
it's never long – a circuit or two
then he leads her back to the creaking chair
fancy-foots it to the kitchen to fetch a glass of water
while she mops a scarlet face
with a limp hanky

like I say... I love to see them dance
reminds me to play my bass more tenderly
even the most cumbersome creations
can surprise with an elegant arpeggio

Natalie
By Hunter Armstrong

Martin stood in front of the long bathroom mirror. What he saw did not give him the rush of pleasure he would once have gained from viewing his former sleek, body. He was seventy two years old now, so what did he expect – really? The loose drooping rolls of abdominal skin, the sagging where his biceps used to be, the turkey-wattles under his chin. The reality was almost too much. He looked away, disturbed by the stark negativity of the comparison of himself now and his former being. Out of the bathroom window he could see, as he looked down to the street one floor below, lithe bodies of youth heading towards the beach-front. It set his teeth on edge, the sense of loss he was feeling. Not only had he lost his appearance. He had lost his wife of thirty five years to a raging brain tumour, an event so recent he still woke at night and reached out to touch her. Now he was losing himself.

After dressing, an act that restored some sense of worth as he covered up the more gross elements of change, and checking to see that his hair was neat and his teeth free of the morning's breakfast cereal, he went down stairs to wait for Natalie to arrive. Natalie was his oldest step-daughter and was coming around to collect some of her mother's treasures that had been promised her. Martin felt a frisson of anticipation at seeing Natalie but, at the same time, an intrusion of mild dread at facing her. Twenty years before, Natalie had come back from New Zealand where she had been working for two years and spent six months living with Martin and Susy before going to Adelaide and her new job. In that six months Martin had developed a passion for Natalie that he had been at great pains to suppress. Her daily closeness was almost painful as his desire for her developed. Not only was it an insidious intrusion into his love of and devotion to his wife of twenty years, it occupied his nights with dreams, sexual dreams where he came close to final intimacy Natalie but always was thwarted at the last moment. Natalie's departure, wrenching for Martin as it was at the time, gave him breathing space. It all would have been safe and settled if he hadn't made that phone call to her. Natalie's response was to let her mother know what a deceiver Martin had turned out to be. All Martin had wanted to do was to be honest with Natalie. He told her of the one-sidedness of his feelings and mused on the possibility of fulfilment had the circumstances and the timing been different. Fortunately Natalie cooled down and decided to leave her mother unaware of Martin's confession.

The door chimes rang out. Martin got to his feet and idled

reluctantly towards the door. Would this be the last time he would see Natalie? Given the run of circumstances it would be the most likely outcome. He would do his best to savour the experience. If only she would show some warmth to him the occasion could end up being pleasantly memorable. That was all he might hope for.

Martin opened the door. Natalie stood there, magnetic as ever. "Hullo Martin, may I come in?"

Martin was immediately frozen for conversation. This was his Natalie of old. Forty four years of age but as graceful and electric as always. He found his voice. "Come on in, Natalie. It's really nice to see you."

They went through to the kitchen area. Natalie took the offered seat, facing him as she sat down. She crossed her long legs and as she did Martin caught a glimpse of lace. His mind began to heat up.

"Would you like coffee?"

Receiving an affirmative answer Martin made two lattes.

'How do I start a smooth conversation with her?' he asked himself.

The question needed no answer. Natalie was the first to speak. "I've come for some of mother's things as you know. I know where they are and I'll get them later. But right now I want to talk to you about something that has been bothering me for a long time." Martin began to feel his flesh creep. 'Surely this is not going to be about my huge gaffe of twenty years ago.'

Natalie took a deep breath before continuing. "You will remember the time when I was living here after coming home from New Zealand? You do, don't you?"

'Oh, oh here it comes.' Martin swallowed hard. "I certainly do. And if you want, I'll apologise again and again for the distress that my indiscretion caused you. I was really silly to make that call."

There was a pause. The sea breeze put the curtains into a drift across the kitchen window. Gulls called in the distance. Natalie found her voice. "Ahem – actually it is about your call. Let me explain. You may have noticed how I would sometimes flaunt myself in front of you then, especially when it was only the two of us around. And that behaviour, I am unhappy to say, goes back to my teenage years. I was wary, at first, of your interposition into our family. I was often rude to you, I know. Then, as I was passing through the later stages of adolescence I realised that my attitude was, in part, due to being jealous of my mother. It was a time when I was having trouble connecting with boys. At home it was easy to look at you and imagine that you were my boyfriend. I realise now that in a way I idolised you. Then, when I left school, it was off to University and away from home. In the first three months of first year I was desperately homesick. I missed Mum, my sisters and I missed you. Desperately. Each time I came home I was pleased to be with everybody but especially I was happy to be around you. But you were very busy and were devoting all your free time to Mum. There seemed to be none left for me. So, I decided that my crush on you was a teenage infatuation and tried to rise above it. Graduating and going to New Zealand made it a bit easier. Time passed and I began to immerse myself in my own work – and, of course, in the lives of a series of men. But none of them was as rounded, as complete as my stepfather. So, when I decided to return to Australia and Mum offered me the chance to live at home for a while I was so happy. I was all aflutter about seeing you and being with you again. What changes would two years have wrought? To me you were the same. Subconsciously, I think, I began to draw you in. There were guile-filled tricks and moments of craftiness as I played on your male vulnerability. I was never sure how well I had done. You gave nothing away – at least not until that phone call. When I got it I was stunned – stunned that you had been drawn in so comprehensively."

Natalie drew a deep breath. "So, you can see that I have as much to answer for as you did all those years ago. I gave the signals, you responded and suddenly I was confronted with the need to handle the big fish I seem to have landed. I was terrified. All I could do in defence was to pretend outrage and threaten to reveal all. Thank God I didn't."

Martin felt a cool breeze of relief pass over him. He cleared his throat. "Look, I was doing a silly thing allowing myself to be swept away by your fresh youthfulness. It was not that I was going off your mother. I was in love with her. She meant a great deal to me then. And still does…" A lump-in-the-throat moment overtook Martin. He looked down, head in hands. It was a full minute before he could speak again. "Immediately I got your message about how outraged you were at the meaning of my phone call I wanted to explain the whole thing in greater detail to you in person. But there was no chance to do so. And now twenty years have gone by and I have still been wishing for that moment to be mine – to give you a proper explanation."

Natalie broke in. "Now you can see that there's no need, really. I wished I had had the gumption to speak to you then but I just didn't have it – until now. Do you think you can forgive me for my lack of courage?"

"Only if you can forgive me for my gross ham-handedness. You know I have had a soft spot for you ever since I joined your family when you were a rather demanding ten year old. You fascinated me right from the start and presented me with a real challenge. I just let myself get too involved. So, are you able to forgive and forget?"

"Oh, Martin, that's exactly what I was going to ask." Natalie extended her hand. Martin shook it and smiled.

"Now I'll have a look at those things of mum's."

You Call To Me As Water
By Ronald L Kundinger

You call to me as water
calls to land that ceaseless
intertwining of earth and wave
controlled by moons and seasons
heat and longing the desire
to move beyond boundaries
beyond the contrasts of soft curves and sharp
edges
We move together and yet
are separated by a well defined
razor edge by your constant flowing
you erode me allow bits and pieces
to fall into you darkness changing swiftly
to bright silver
Don't ask me how I know this how each night
as I wade into your depths I know
how to breathe this is a ritual
this baptism this drowning
I claw hand over hand through your current
hoping to be carried to that place where the water
meets the sky and fountains into the light
and you shine
you shine

She Feels Him At A Seaside Motel
By John Karl Stokes

That vicious know-all, fright
            lights up windows
leaps up to watch
         night retake a street
Nothing's changed.

She starts at the pick of
           old dreams
shrinks at shadow voices.

The curves of his buttock
      and the moon

are the same
              as they always were.

All is what it seems.

First published in *Australian Poetry Journal*, 2015.

Puppy Love
By Frank Cardiff

My eyes looked at hers
and her eyes looked at mine
and our hearts seemed to beat extra fast
and I knew - how I knew,
it was true, it was true -
I had fallen in love at last!
Her look was quite modest
and downcast and coy
but she felt just the same, I could tell
then in one reckless moment
I whispered "be mine" -
and I then bought the kennel as well.

Previously published in *The Accidental Poet*

Love
By Frank Meintjies

   ... sewn

      in the tiered hills of kwazulu-natal, occasionally countered
      where thoughts cling, just beyond cramped dwellings; there were

   floods

there were winds
at times
fires flared, flames like flags

by watersheds, windbreaks, singed limbs
gaps that let in light; reactivated buds
deeply etched days & spun moments, sprouting
from quotidian years

   you arrive
   like a phantom from the mist
   tending, remaking, conjuring; sprinkling spores

from this, from these scenes
behold, something light
playful and at once potent and awe-laden
germinates

Musings
By Katie Lewington

What do I know about love
aged twenty years and seven months?

that it becomes a word, often
spoken but with less
significance than it did
when I was not in love
a word to use, cherish
bind together
two lovers
romance and communication
become important -
love is a given.

My Form Of Loving
By Alasdair S. Goudie

An unhealthy, jagged obsession.
Anglo boy in a Celtic school,
Learn to keep one's head down.
Bide one's time and bite one's tongue.
The urges, as they come to all, must
Be suppressed.
For no girl would ever have you.
Or boy, for though the year may be modern,
These hills are old.
I could not love another,
And so never loved me.

It is an unhealthy construct.
Friend, mother, dream-time lover,
Have said as much to me.
Informed me again of therapy,
But there was nothing wrong with me,
As fuelled, jaded eyes could see.

For I found it twice upon a screen.
A loving girl, one week, one year,
In which I became bolstered.
My virtues extolled, my positives compounded
At last, I thought, someone loving me.
But inside, still, my deprivation
Stopped me from loving me.

Fat, dumb,
Nerdy, whiny,
All these thoughts returned again.
Affixed became I to keyboard's haven.
But they could not replace my heart
Nor keep it, in the end.
Nor could I keep theirs.
All the accounts would flick offline
My parents there another time
To mop up fresh, sourceless tears
Of ceaselessly vacant origin.

My desperation kept me in.
Kept us angry, even when

An ocean could have drown our rage.
Jealously floods back in
Whenever lights flick off and then
Imaginations run wild again
Inferiority flood in again.
To love someone through a webcam
Breaks my brittle heart again.

And still the list and time increased.
For I required them, my lens
A bedrock I would extol to them
But I built my home from their cherished love.
And when it fled,
However brief,
I ran, as madman, through these glens
Howling with spirit bereft anew
As I flung my mind upon the fire
And seared the faults deeper still
Why there could never be another was all within my broken brain.

I deified them in their absence,
Regardless of their numerous faults
This sank me further, down below
Until all given light from others dappled away
And my ennui entombed me again.

Recently, though, another ended.
A better one than all before.
And as we detached with better grace,
I saw, clearer, my lives afore.

My bitter, erring, lack of mind.
My self-esteem in distant other's hands
How I spurned the constancy of my mother
For fleeting strolls on stranger's sands.

So now, at last, I move along.
Within this time I cannot see
My purposes,
But now I know.
In time,
I'll begin loving me.

Desolations Ancient Waste
By David Hollywood

Desolations Ancient Waste,
And where is my love now?
"Gone"….. Says the past,
And shrouds the setting sun.

Darkness! Concepts,
Who shall take my face?
And who'll replace,
To make my steps,
With you beside them now.

My fears he to,
Becomes for you,
Your constant love, anew,
In terms foregone,
My actions long,
To be him loved and true.

Beside my prize,
Regrets my eyes,
Were nere disguised,
Through which you came to, knew,
That if I had, just covered up,
Our times would never grew,
And pain would not be new.

And not to be, so dearly loved,
Would shield my heart from break,
If stead a happiness of bliss,
So ignorant, of more than this,
Would temper sense, reduce, forsake,
Due to the heights unreached,
And would my life be blessed, unteached,
For never knowing you?

I cannot give my past back more,
Than knowing you loved me,
So if the strap crossed chest, my pain,
Continues to be taut,
Constricted strife,
So is my life,

Trussed, bound and feeling fraught,
A crushing with the strain.

But never would I change the sore -
Or ever swap you for?
An ease restrained,
A life more saned,
A grief not known, for you.

I know I've searched, and shall again,
For views of all to come,
Eternity, shall take my fall,
And go forever to,
A view I hope,
May bring you then,
Into my essence, when
No longer have I got to choke,
Upon this loss of you.

Where in the earth,
Cannot be found,
An excavated heart,
All ruined, fall,
Neath toppled ground,
Fore early splendid mirth,
Until that time,
Knows no de-part,
Cause happy was its birth,
But then came still,
My life to fill,
Obscured by tumbled grief,
And searched a place,
To hide my face,
Lay, restless underneath,
Events, these wounds untimely scrape,
Surprised with out escape,
Before it took and razed me low,
As love of you,
Peer's barren now,
And all my past, my statures last,
Is gone to take its place,
My time has lapsed
To die its cast
Eternal in its rest.

Followed thoughts of your depart,
Has left a withered scene,
Of hopes we'd had and cherished heart,
Ideals, no longer deemed,
And taken of, from all its grace,
I look onto the place,
Where hallowed you were queen,
Instead of stabbed, a royal pierce,
Into the peace,
At holy templed scene,
And now our bloods I feel it through,
The grape where once were you,
A punctured stead is trickling dew,
In reddened shades and hue,
In places kept,
Just sacred all for you.
Your pedestal I cracked, I knew,
When stumbling at the fall,
I built on high,
My hearts revere,
And sensed it was my fault,
To be so sure of you.
My tortures call,
My memories tore,
At all we'd planned to be,
Where nothing else could last,
But certainty of us,
Eternal to the last,
Created up into the sky,
A dome where only you,
Would be for me,
For sure my faith believed,
Because you said we'd last.

So what of plans on top of when,
I'd only thought with you,
That futures been,
To us a past, of when,
We lived it through.
Instead now present plans askew,
Turn round upon the mask,
And looking back in order to,
Perceive the view,
No longer lives it's course,
And stead it goes into,

A void, where now I can't see you.

My love for you,
So hard it tempts,
To try a new life's worth,
Without!
But stead not able, being banished,
Choking, gasp, it through,
I fear that aft it's finished, end,
I will instead just vanish.
I am convinced a couples song,
Can journey long,
And become so rare,
That only those who broke their life,
Will ever know compare,
As represents, so few, my strife,
I come no more to know,
Because my love, decided send,
Me oft while she can mend,
Into some place, she cannot fare,
It tokens then my end.

Tiny Bud
By Angharad Thompson Rees

Tiny bud
Red Glow
As petals open
Gentle
Slow
A glimpse of nature's
fragrant play
On my lips
my skin
my mind you stay
As ink stained
pollen from your
inner gold
pierces my skin
with your tender hold
I pray these
petals in full
bloom
won't whither
to nothing
and decay
too soon
My tiny bud
Your red glow
My heart you opened
Gentle
Slow

Wet And Wild
By Dayle Ashton

Here I am again,
Standing at the top
Of the highest
Waterslide in the park,
Looking at the dizzy height
That makes my heart stop,
Last time I swore
I would never come back
After ending up
So battered and bruised,
Until you took my hand,
Bringing me to this spot
With a peaceful feeling,
So here I am,
Taking it to the limit
One more time,
I know you won't let me down,
So I close my eyes,
Step over the edge
And freefall into your arms.

Tender Reeds By the River
By Akwu Sunday Victor

For my mother, Alice Sunday and all mothers all over the world on mothers' day, May, 2016

That tinkling sensation that comes with much sunlight
Those beads of sweat that break on the forehead,
When the sun lashes the earth and all in it...

I harken to the spirit, that inward referee
And like the wild bird and Ralia or Simbi in the grove
I follow the footfalls of the spirit into the palm tree grove

The birds singing in the woods, sang unknown songs
I tilt my ears, like the dial of a radio, filtering the breeze
Endless chattering, to pick the rhythm of the songs in the wood

At the mouth of the street, a jagged stone stood
Upon it I took my place and down the heart of the flowing fluid
Fishes swim against the flowing fluid flipping tiny filaments

Then like the flash of light, like the dazzling of broken glass
In the sand, it came, the thought of them, the thought came
And my heart began to sing, accompanied by the drums of the stream

The trees that filled the earth with seeds, I recall to mind
Nights of pains and agony as the pod of blood formed
Taking shape, like a painting on a painter's table evolving

Motion slowed as another being takes away the primordial
Freedom of the limbs, lips like the wings of a trapped butterfly
Tremble as the clod of blood nibble at the pot of life

And their portraiture fill my imagination, nameless pains
Gnaw the flesh of my heart, like soldiers charging into the arena
Of death unperturbed, they enter the theatre of new life

Faces contorted, form distorted by the burden borne
And between the earth and the heavens, their breath lingers
And to some it returns and to others gone with the wind forever

This is the journey taken to bring forth beings in being
But then, a moment is often not taken, in life's orangery

To reflect upon this sacrifice of blood, of life and death

And now in the palm grove, with the birds in the trees
And the trees, like drunken men, or possessed priests
Of a forgotten deity, dance shaking their massive heads

And now in the palm grove, with the stream tingling my ears
Caressing the sole of my soul, I see like on a screen
The essence of sacrifice, the meaning of love

And the spirit whispers in my ears, this tender song
And I began to sing right from the grove of palm trees
And the wind came, like a dove and took my voice to the orb's end

Pockets Of The Heart
By Ella Edwards

The heart is the most wonderful organ, our very soul.
Where we have love and heartbreak and it keeps us whole.
The very centre of our being, and of our very existence.
In friendship and love, it really lowers our resistance.

But no matter how much we love, our heart we can't fill.
We can say our heart overflows and can even spill,
but there is always room for more admiration and caring,
our feelings of adoration, we are forever sharing.

That's why it must be, we have pockets in our hearts.
that no one else can fill. Like lines drawn on charts,
we have one for Mum one for Dad and one for Nan and Pop,
siblings and cousins and friends, they sure mean a lot.

Of course the love extends to god, faith and beautiful pets,
those you can love unconditionally, and with no regrets.
The pockets in your heart are like airbags that expand.
Unique pockets, the whole thing just makes you feel grand.

As we meet someone special to love, to live your life with,
your heart fills and fills with love, you know its no myth,
it feels as your heart, will beat right out of your chest,
and wonder what you have done, to feel so exquisitely blessed.

Your heart fills with this new love, it's brimming.
Love is all you can think about, your heart is swimming.
But when you stop to take a breath, the pockets in your heart
remind you they are there, more love simply fills your beating part.

And even though your heart feels it is full to saturation.
A child - a miracle, another of gods wonderful creations.
Yet again a pocket expands for each one that is born.
Endless love, your marvellous heart simply adorns.

In someone's heart, is truly a wonderful place to be,
to fit into one of those special pockets, you must agree.
The more pockets you fill, the more pockets you share.
Gives you more love, till you have love to spare.

So live your lives, filling those expanding pockets with love.

Your heart wont burst, each will grow like a rubber glove.
You can feel it inside, that feeling of only love, treasure
the pockets in your heart. They'll bring you much pleasure.

The Names
By Zahra Zuhair

I know Aylan Kurdi
and the others who came
but didn't live,
to see the end of this game.

Game makers,
in your fancy suits,
The floor is red
but you wear boots.

I know my sisters,
Noor, Raneem and Najla.
and my brothers, Baalousha and Aslan,
Almataouq, Aashoor and Jumaa.

Game makers,
you cannot run forever,
the lives you have taken
will be avenged by another.

I cannot join them
but I know the freedom fighters;
young Ahed Tamimi,
Rachel Corrie and the others.

I have no weapons with me;
I have everything to lose
but I also have my prayers and my love,
and I have my words and my views.

If that is all I have,
then that is what I will give,
because they are fighting death
while I live.

Previously published: *Keeeptalking.wordpress.com*

Memories Rekindled
By David Watt

I loved her once and swore our love was true
And would have loved her still instead of rue,
Her loss in reckless sentiment of youth
When callowness transcended spoken truth.

What tenderness and passion shared beget;
I knew it then and I will know it yet,
Regardless of the course I have to chart
Retracing footsteps leading to her heart.

To South, to East, to North and then to West
No other face compares, for hers is best;
And never since has aimless idle talk
Been prized as on those days we used to walk.

And nights we held in passionate embrace
Have left their mark indelible to trace;
Each contour guiding surely as it must
While embers glow, ere ashes blow to dust.

Time for love is perilously short,
But real emotion never comes to naught
As long as memories amorous take flight
On way from precious day and treasured night.

How Could I Fail To See?
By Kariuki wa Nyamu

Neema,

How could I fail to see
the just right timing of
our budding affection?

How could I fail to see
the immensity of adoration
embedded in our interactions?

How could I fail to see
the patient waiting for each other
to get done with school?

How could I fail to see
you weren't the usual urban girl
whose ways are not up to scratch?

How could I fail to see
you and I inserting gold rings
into each other's finger?

How could I fail to see
we could modestly put up
with each other's flaws?

How could I fail to see
the likely strength of our matrimony
till the end of Time?

How could I fail to see
that our household could
turn out an envy of many?

How could I fail to see
your affability, chastity,
moderation and industry?

How could I fail to see
that your African gorgeousness
could eternally charm me?

Anyhow Neema dear,
you'll have to pardon me
for fruitfully failing
to put in the picture
what the future holds
after all,
I'm just
a man.

First published on *Dwartonline* literary blog on 16th May 2016

Splashdown
By Helen Bowers

When we were lovers...
we orbited reality from an unsafe distance
spaced out satellites looking down
on Mount Olympus

When we were...
swimming in concentric circles
diving deep, awash with dreams,
near-drowning in a storm-tossed reach
of the Sea of Tranquillity

When we...
came down to earth hyperventilating
followed by the usual debriefing –
nice place to visit
wouldn't want to live there

When -

Stolen
By Cath Bore

In the dance hall he takes Helen into his arms. Her hair smells of apricots, soft against his cheek. Such sweet grey eyes, they make his wits quicken and sharpen like morning frost. He knows he should mention that the top button of her cotton print dress is undone but instead sneaks a peek, humming into her hair as they dance. The lights come up. That's a shame. He prefers the lights dimmed, low and gentle.

Feet trot on tiles. Heels click out of time. The mashed potato, the shag, he knows all the dances, wants to do each with Helen but she murmurs his name and adds 'you'll have to leave.' Grey eyes turn stern blue, icy not sweet. 'I'm sorry,' she says to the people watching. 'This gentleman is known to us.' He blinks.

He's not in the dance hall anymore. This mardy cold woman, she is not Helen.

He is marched out of the supermarket, but pushes an apricot into his pocket first. Walk it off, he's told.

What, walk off the apricot? He slouches, legs as heavy as wet sand but in his head he waltzes home, both feet in a percussive shuffle, arms full of warm.

The stolen fruit bumps gently against his hip.

Motivation
By Rosie Mapplebeck

He always said "if you
    were to stray
        it would mean the end of us"

he'd been there before, never
understood her drives
her pleas to be heard

he never understood my pleas
to be heard,
    to have drive
        so i strayed
            from his way
                to be loved

Sushi For Tea
By Trudy Duffy - Wigman

Looking at the supermarket competition form, I hesitate. Will I use my own name? Apart from my best friend Tammy, nobody uses my name anymore. Letters that come through the letterbox are addressed to Mr and Mrs Sean Lynch. I am Mrs Sean Lynch. On the form, you have to answer a question about oranges and the first prize is a cruise to the Mediterranean. Fourteen days for two, with full board on a luxury cruise liner, calling at ports in Italy, Spain, Malta and Greece. Imagine...

The nearest I ever got to a cruise was the ferry from Dun Laoghaire to Holyhead, when we were going to a guest-house in Blackpool on our honeymoon. We were very excited about going abroad, even if it was only England. For most of the journey we stood at the railing, holding hands. When the boat had docked, we took a train to Blackpool, eating sandwiches and drinking from little bottles of juice that Sean bought in a kiosk. I had never bought ready-made sandwiches before and it made me feel pampered. A sandwich in my family was a slab of brown bread with a chunk of cheese, wrapped in grease-proof paper.

The train journey went far too quick for my liking. Blackpool was magic. Our guest-house was tucked away in a side street, close to the beach. The smell of kippers and fried eggs for breakfast hung in the reception area.

I felt thrilled by entering our name in the guest book: Mr and Mrs Sean Lynch. My new name: Mrs Sean Lynch. I could not stop giggling. Our landlady for the week looked at us over her glasses and I began to blush.

'We're just married,' said Sean and I blushed even deeper.

'High tea will be at five thirty sharp. I hope you enjoy your stay here, Mr and Mrs Lynch.'

Sean now calls me: 'y'rself', or 'y'r ma', but in those days he would call me 'my Rose', and 'my love'. Or other names, when we lay cuddling on the big double bed. Then the children came along and the big bed became a place where stories were read, tears were dried and noses blown. I became a mother with my first-born; I became 'ma' in the years to follow.

Halfway down the aisle, between the cheeses and the meats, I hear a woman speaking to the manager. She wears a lovely coat that must have cost a few bob. She has the figure for it. Unlike me.

'Have you got any sushi?' she asks.

I look at the meats and wonder what to get for tea. Macaroni cheese, perhaps, or a fry-up. Sushi..., I had sushi once. Last summer there was an international food festival in the market square in the Temple Bar area. There were stalls with foods from all over the world. I went early, on my own of course. Sean is more the bacon-and-eggs type of man. The children are not at all interested in anything remotely more exotic then pizza but I read the magazines at the hairdressers, and I know about foreign foods. I tasted tapas from Spain and duck from China and cheese from France that smelled like the laundry basket on Friday.

Sushi were little fishy bites made with sticky sour rice rolled in something that tasted like black rice paper. Nothing much to it, but it seems to be very fashionable nowadays.

Why does she want sushi? It is Friday; perhaps she's having a couple of friends over for drinks and nibbles. They will drink cold white wine from long stemmed glasses and eat little bites: fancy nuts, savoury biscuits, olives and sushi. They will have conversations about books they've read and music they have heard. I will sit on the settee, watching telly and eating a packet of cheese-and-onion crisps, washed away with a can of lager. Himself may or may not join me.

We used to have friends over when we were just married. Sean would invite Kevin, a mate from work, and his wife Tammy. The men used to drink stout; Tammy and I preferred a cider. I'd made a nice spread, with cocktail sausages and tiny sandwiches. We would talk, about the cost of living, the situation in the North and watch Gay Burn in the *Late Late Show*. Tammy and I were pregnant with our first babies at the same time. Together we pushed our trolleys through this supermarket, laden with nappies and baby food. Tammy doesn't come as often anymore; not since she and Kevin were divorced.

The sausages are on special offer so I settle for a nice fry-up with a few rashers, sausages and an egg. Sean can go to the chippy to pick up fries. I'll buy a couple of cans of beer - perhaps he'll stay at home and watch telly with me instead of going to his local. There is a film on and then after that it is Pat Kenny, though the 'Late Late Show' is not the same since Gay Burn quit.

The doctor told me I should be eating salads and low-fat foods. During the week I try, but not in the weekend. I don't get many treats nowadays. The sausages look rather

pale and limp. Perhaps sushi is good for your love life. God knows we can use a bit of help in that direction. All those years ago, in Blackpool, we could not get enough of each other.

After a walk on the beach we'd tiptoe up the stairs to our small bedroom, then turned up for meals slightly late and very flushed. I know all about flushes now. I usually get one between the detergents and the pet food, must be something that triggers it off in the soap smells.

'Oh! Excuse me please!'

My trolley has collided with another. It is the sushi woman.

'I can be such an eejit when I'm in a hurry,' she says. We disentangle our shopping bags and cause a little traffic jam in the aisle. 'Sorry for that!'

She smiles. A nice smile. I don't know what to say, really.

'No harm done. Friday is always a lousy day for shopping anyway.'

From close up, the woman looks frazzled and her hair is a mess. Perhaps she has hot flushes too. In her trolley I spot a packet of green lettuce ('rabbit's food', himself would call it), chicken, a packet of sushi and a bottle of white wine, along with a tub of olives. The kind of food you eat when you have a representative job. I never had a job, let alone a representative one. The kids and the house, that was my work and I did it with pride and joy. She has no children. No one with that kind of food in a supermarket trolley has children.

My children are growing up fast. Ailish, the eldest, is walking out with a very nice young man. Sean and I expect an announcement any day now. Ailish has a university degree and is very bright. She will have babies and a job. Then there is Tony. He has just started college and still lives at home. He is the son every mother wants. Mary is the baby in the house. Cheeky and pretty, she winds her dad around her finger. He calls her 'Princess' and never refuses her anything.

In between Tony and Mary I had three more babies. I lost two and one died within an hour after birth. Every time I walk past the baby food and the nappies, I feel those babies. Sean has never forgotten about them either. Every year around this time he lights a candle in church and without saying anything, he buys me a bunch of flowers. Gerald would have been seventeen this very day. Still, we have been blessed with three fine and healthy children, what is more than a lot of folk can hope for. We went through a rough patch then, Sean and me, blaming something, somebody, God, each other. In the end we stuck together, mainly for the children. And then Mary came along.

Time to hurry. The queues at the checkout are getting longer. I put a six-pack of beer, two cans of cider and a large packet of crisps, plus all the ingredients for a fry-up in my trolley, adding a cucumber and some tomatoes for a salad and tub of ice cream for the children. After all, it is the weekend. In the queue, I get to stand behind the sushi woman. She has succumbed to a very large chocolate bar. She sees me looking and smiles her nice but tired smile. I smile back. She has probably her own things to worry about. I don't envy her really, with her fancy job and her trim figure. I'd rather have sausages than sushi, and a night on the settee with

Sean.

Tràigh Mhòr
By Karin Slater

Where we camped
there is a patch of grass
not quite square
already yellowed
and a sequence of holes
small and brown
where the pegs
that held us in
kept out the night
you made me warm
pulled me closer
along the tarpaulin base
in sleeping bags
to make the same
shape as you.

Previously published in *New Writing Scotland 29* in 2011

Do You Believe In Soul Mates
By Nikita Krishna Kumar

"Do you believe in soul mates?", he asked, pouring the honey lemon tea in my favourite mug.

"No, I don't believe in soul mates. Yes, I do believe that there is someone made for everyone. Someone who walks with you through life." I said, as I made room next to him on the leather sofa.

Room.

Right where there is always a place for me. A place kept for me. I loved talking to him. Love rather. A past tense somehow does not fit the vibe he gives to me. I like him near, even when he is not near. Talking about perspectives is what created an interest between the two of us. We find each other fascinating. Always something new to find out. We lie too much, not the kind that can be called deceiving. We lie about just how much we love each other. It's a test. For both.

The only thing we are, is, Real. Real as people. Real as individuals.

I continued further on my statement, "But I believe more in the fact that I fell in love with you and I will make every effort to make us work, only because I don't have any reason why I shouldn't. You make me happy and I don't need a tag to the point of calling you a soul mate. You are just YOU. Real. Perfectly sexy."

He looked at me with that mischievous little grin, the one I found involuntarily and mysteriously sexy.

"What?" I looked up at him from the crook of his arm.

"Well, wouldn't calling us "Soulmates" be sort of like a movie for you?" he asked, very seriously. But he would never believe something like that.

I reached and kissed him to let him know "The Force" is real.

"Aren't we all living our very own Movie every day? This is a story. I'm living my story," I said as I turned over clutching his arm.

He adjust himself just the right amount till our legs interlock and our fingers intertwine. He whispers in my ear: "You're always going to be my Panda."

Flair to Share
By Catherine Morgans

She has a way about her
The experience of a long life
A heart with wings
The making of glamour
And style of Paris in spring

She has a way about her
Her family of home
And steadfast connections
Turning her way
Building a pyramid of stone

She has a way about her
All by her design
Without doubt or fear
Speaking her mind
Putting in place those dear

She has a way about her
The twinkle of her eyes
A cheeky smile to surprise
Then mention of colour and style
Will set her flying high

She has a way about her
Don't mess with her plans
She might take your breath
Sharp wit and charm
Aiming to please her legion of fans

She has a way about her
Enclosed in her arms
The world she touches
Embracing each lesson
Finding the stars within her clutches

The Tone Of Your Voice
By Martin Redfern

I watch you answer the phone.
From the tone of your voice,
I realise it's over.

I hear the tenderness
I had understood was mine.
You run your fingers through your hair,
The breeze unsettling your dress.
I comb your exquisite face
To search for hope.
But your eyes are exuberant now,
You overflow with him.

I want to plead for what we once had -
Instead I say nothing.
How do I tell you what you have told me?

Baby
By Kathleen Coyle

'Don't worry, Baby. I won't let them take you.'

I rubbed the cloth in small, soothing motions around her sides, and finished with a single sweep along her keys. She was spotless. But still, this feeling of agitation refused to shift.

My eyes flickered to the crisp, yellow pages peeking out of the box beside the piano. I leaned over and removed the book with both hands, as though handling some precious ornament. 'You must take care of me', declared the hard, musical document, 'in exchange, for the secrets of the old world.'

Written with my mother's fingers was a stack of grey numbers: 1-3-5. I ran my own forefinger over the scrawls, but with a pang, felt only the smoothness of the page. I considered the writing again, and wondered: what would the day have been like?

I played a few notes in the hope of awakening this secret. It was probably winter. While father fought through the snow to make it to work, she was holed up and safe in the house, with me. But I was asleep in my crib: she was using this precious quiet time to teach herself a new song. I looked at the page again, and it seemed to whisper, 'No, it was a summer's day...' I could see the light falling into the room, a single stripe along the piano, across her tawny brown mane. I exhaled, and shifted on the stool as my hair tickled my back.

'Abby.' His voice echoed around the room.

My hands froze. I looked up and saw my father staring back at me.

I cleared my throat. 'I was just... '

'Clair de Lune,' he finished, walking towards me. 'I haven't seen that piece out in a long time.'

He settled one hand on my shoulder, and with the other, inspected my cut up fingertips. I flinched, and looked at the red smudge imprinted on the keys. 'What have I told you... you have to stop playing so hard.'

I felt his hand slip off my shoulder.

'I don't know how else to... ' I trailed off, as he walked away. Looking from the piano, to the padlocked box that marked the only furniture in the room, I already knew where he was going.

'Do you have to?'

He slammed the box shut, as he turned to me, with the spanner in his hand.

'Abby, you know it has to be done. How else am I going to feed us? Heat us?'

I met his eyes. For a moment we both considered the space where the dining table had been, before he left the room, and inevitably made his way to the bottom of the garden.

****

I remember the first time he took me down to the shed. The light was broken, but I could still make out the pianos, one piled on top of the other. A Steinway now characterised by its fading, toothy-yellow keys; two upright (vertical) Bechsteins, whose similar shape made occupying the same, small space difficult; and a shiny black Yamaha.

All different, all bound for the slaughter.

Although this was the third economic crash, it was the first that had rendered the world unrecognisable. The demand for every run of the mill, corporate job, had diminished. Now, it was only the work that people needed to survive, that everyone from bakers to ex-bankers had found themselves taking on.

Ding-dong.

I opened the door, and found Mr. Valentine, father's ex-colleague and friend, standing on the other side of the threshold. He always had the same whiskery moustache and a scabby bowler hat, to cover his bald head.

Calling father from in from the garden, I offered to make tea.

'It's only the basic teabags... with the rations,' I explained.

Mr Valentine's hat was nodding. I went into the kitchen and sorted through the mugs that had the least amount of chips. I waited for the water to boil on the stove and stared into the empty space where the kettle had been.

'I just wonder...' Father was saying, 'perhaps I could still find some way to repair her.'

I hurriedly made the tea, and returned to the room, where Father had arranged all of the cushions we owned into three separate piles: three seats each. Father had already claimed one, while Mr Valentine remained standing.

'Repair who?' I said. The teacup shivered in its saucer as I passed it to Mr. Valentine.

'Darling, we were just talking about Baby. How - she's got very old, and...'

'She belonged to my grandmother' I shot back. 'And then my mother. It's not up to you.'

'Repairing her would be far too expensive...' tried Mr. Valentine. He adopted a sympathetic look, for my father's sake. 'A labour of love, more than anything else. And you can't afford it. At least this way, you can make a good... profit, out of her. Sell her on for wood and...'

'No.'

Father exchanged looks with Mr. Valentine. My voice had sounded outside of myself.

Brave.

Father walked over to the fire and reached into the wood basket. As he picked up a raggedy piece of our dining table, a discoloured piece of wood was revealed underneath. The same, smooth texture as the Bechstein he'd brought in last week.

'Surely you've heard,' continued Mr Valentine. 'They've started raiding homes. If word gets out that you have such a valuable piece...'

'Those are baseless scare stories,' Father interjected, casting a look towards me.

Seeming to miss the point, Mr. Valentine continued. 'And besides... the baby grand was probably never completely intact anyway.'

I could feel myself desperately trying to hold all the pieces of myself together at once. 'She is PER-FECT-LY intact,' I said, my voice rising to a crescendo. 'When are you going to realise that pianos aren't just fodder for whenever YOU bankers decide to screw up the world?'

'Abby, control your temper,' my father's word was a staccatoed warning. 'This was what I was telling you about...' he said looking at Mr. Valentine. At me.

'You need help.'

I blinked back at him. 'Well this... isn't... helping,' I protested, my voice breaking. 'What would mother... have said?'

'Your mother loved that piano. But she loved you more, and it is my responsibility to look after you.' I shook the tears from my face, feeling no choice but to leave the room. As I walked out, I heard Mr. Valentine quietly saying: 'It's a hard decision to make over a piano.' I stopped, listening. 'Can't you... at least get someone else to do it, if the time comes?'

'It would be dangerous. Loosening the strings... it'll take a long time. There's too much tension in them. They have to be unwound slowly, and... I'll have to do it.'

I ran upstairs and drifted into sleep, after a long episode of sobbing about the prospect of losing my mother all over again.

I woke without an alarm. Sunlight peeked in at me from behind the curtain, but I couldn't match its encouragement. Instead, I stayed in the same, fetal position, until I heard a door opening. I looked at the clock:

Five to eight.

Finding the courage to slip on my dressing gown and move

downstairs, I walked into the workshop and stopped, paralysed.

Her black lid had already been removed.

Most of her keys were gone and father was crouched over the cast-iron plate, whose pins held two hundred and twenty-two strings. He removed the first pin, and with it, the string unfurled with all the songs that had accumulated over the years. Why couldn't I stop it?

I watched him unpick each pin from her string one by one. And after a while a strange thing happened; it started to feel cathartic, rather than upsetting. There was nothing I could do, or would do, because I knew that father was doing the best that he could do for us without my mother, without his wife.

As he finally reached over to separate the cast-iron plate from the soundboard, I realised that Mr. Valentine had been right; like so many pianos that had been hurriedly meshed together to satisfy demand in the 1800s, Baby didn't fit perfectly. But, she had helped my mother to teach me the strange, and wonderful effect music has on our bodies, and the extraordinary bonds we form with our instruments: she was the last tangible link.

But now father had reached the final stage: he began removing the ribs from the soundboard, first slowly and carefully, then more frantically, until I realised that he had tears streaming down his face. His upper body shook as he tried to detach the next rib, but unsteady hands wouldn't allow it. I rushed over.

'Abby...' he whined, looking at something behind the piano. I turned, and saw the verdict etched onto the piece of wood that he had dismantled: Yamaha. Not Baby.

'I couldn't, Abby.' I rushed over, and drew him into my cheek for an embrace that was long overdue, aware that his tears were mingling with mine. 'I can't, anymore.'

Afterwards, we sat in the front room. Everything was quiet this time; from the way we settled our teacups onto the floor, to the lack of noise from outside.

He poured another cup, and I passed him the jug of milk. He took a spoonful of sugar and began stirring it round.

'We'll stay with Mr. Valentine from a while. We might all be poor, but he's the richest of us all; he has an empty room that you can keep Baby in. We can decide on the next step after that.'

I was still suspicious about Mr. Valentine's intentions, but now wasn't the time for debate. I nodded, pouring a second cup for myself, too.

'Did I tell you about the time I restored a piano?' my father said.

'I don't think so.'

'It was before your mother got sick. The neighbour wanted to restore a piano that had grown up through the family for years, like yours, and his little girl, Eve was her name, had always wanted to be able to play. Well, and your mother knew how I used to watch your grandfather restore pianos day in, day out...'

I smiled, knowing I was seeing the insides of something that rarely appeared.

'I remember the morning that I brought the piano over. They said that without realising it they had forgotten what it was to see their daughter happy, until that moment. I felt part of this important, family occasion and they were right. She did have the most beautiful smile.'

'And what about the piano? I asked. 'Did it smile?'

My father lifted the cup to his lips. 'I don't know,' he said. His expression was sincere. 'It might have.'

To Get Close To You
By Dayle Ashton

I am looking
For something
To fill my senses,
While time is still turning,
To get as close
As I can be to you
With all that I have to give,
I you could only hear me speak
Of these dreams as they escape
Through my fingers,
You might take me in your arms,
Give me the key to your door,
Open your heart,
Lead me to your bed,
Show me there is no tomorrow
Before it disappears forever
With the birds in the wind,
Leaving my heart and soul
Aching for your touch.

Xanthippe
By Pab Roberts

Once upon a nightingale
Sweetness and light
My song was hers forever
And for long did I yearn
To touch her emotions so

The man she chose over me
Was cruel, he laughed at grace
She couldn't see further than
His charming smile
And so my soul frustrated

But then again I met once more
My soft gay abandoned lass
Her hair as gossamer
greyly encircling disappointment

And as I gazed into those lovelorn eyes
To stretch past the ice of wasted years
I saw my sweet Xanthippe

Kiss
By Kimmy Alan

Not a word was said
Between lovers transfixed
Save the sound of their kiss
No other acoustics
Can grant such bliss

Seven Years Four Days Eleven Months
By Rachel Walker

She missed his presence every day. The flat was empty and cold; it stank of Supernoodles and lentil soup because she had never learned to cook. She kept forgetting to buy milk and biscuits and she never remembered to set her alarm. She had tried – but it was useless. The shop was always shut by the time she got there and she was still in the habit of waking up too late, cramming toast into her mouth as she frantically tried to organise herself.

She missed the days of having milky cereal every morning. She missed waking up to the reassuring splatter of the shower; she missed coming home from work and being greeted with enticing aromas and meals that didn't arrive crunchy in a plastic packet. She felt alone. She was alone – singing to herself as she tackled the clinging stains on the bowls and plates and cutlery that littered her kitchen; commenting aloud on the ludicrous plot twists in her favourite TV shows, receiving no sarcastic criticism of how noisily she chewed her popcorn. It didn't dispel the loneliness, these feeble attempts. It didn't make her want to stifle the tears that bubbled up when she noticed the half-filled bookcases, sterile and plain. And the drawers, once so crammed with intermingling socks and underwear. There was a pale gap on the wall where his poster of The Godfather had hung, for four years, and the clutter on her side of their shared desk was no longer restrained, no longer subdued by his perpetual efforts to rein in her messiness.

It was liberating in a way, she supposed. The intensity was gone and now she could live normally and impulsively; unhampered. She let her shoes clog up the hall and she stayed out too late, drinking tequila and pitchers in some student bar, dismissive of her 9am start the next morning. She sobbed unashamedly at tragically romantic films, unimpeded by his disparaging looks, and she blasted rap music when she brushed her hair in the morning. She didn't have to pretend to appreciate gloomy classical symphonies or violent gangster films where everyone ended up bloody and dead. It was exhilarating – like moving away from your parents for the first time, like being a selfish teenager all over again. She had her friends round, for gin and salacious gossip, and it was miraculous, really, not having to usher them out at precisely eleven or to contend with interminable moaning about how he had had to watch the football on his erratic iPad. Everyone had commented: she looked so happy, she looked like she was having the time of her life, she was so fun again. No more half-joking enquiries about when they were going to hurry up and get engaged (it had been five years, didn't she know?), no more infuriating jibes about how they were going to be the first to have lots of bouncing babies.

"I'm not sure I want children," she had said repeatedly; endlessly, it seemed. Invariably greeted with smugness – us mummies know best. They had talked about it, a lot. About marriage too. About changing her name and who would be the primary caretaker of the tiny little thing that had begun to chip away at their relationship. He grew keener as time went on; she became less certain. They went away to Paris for their six years' anniversary and walked beneath the Eiffel Tower and she had cried on the balcony, late at night, when he was sleeping. She had begun to miss him even then.

Coast Road
By Kathleen Bleakley

Things set in tar
can vanish
sea-spray
on rocks.

This road
I've told stories

cycled to the coke works
sketched their charcoal beauty

run from coal faces
to rock pools
photographed giant crabs

had moonshine flings
on the beach
after too much wine

navigated the edges
before light and
learned to drive.

The road has closed
now we lean
into the bend
into the curve
of each other
watch for falling rocks
and the opening
of Seacliff Bridge

Previously published in *Lighseekers*, Poetry by Kathleen Bleakley & Images by 'pling, Ginninderra Press, 2015

Exotic Love
By Jacky Perez

Negombo-an exotic name
Yet an unremarkable Sri Lankan city.
The irony -
A faint smile reaches her lips.

He mistakes her interest,
His smile brightens,
His chatter more enthusiastic,
His joy palpable.

But her eyes stray
And rest on the sunset -
A fiery red orange ball
Slowly sinking into the ocean.

He remains oblivious,
Prattling on and on,
Leisurely sipping his Lion Stout,
Love radiating from his eyes.

She is engrossed in her thoughts,
Deaf to the the love in his voice,
Blind to everything but the sun,
Devoid of any feelings.

Their relationship-an exotic match,
But a boy is a boy
And a girl is a girl.
Even in Negombo.

Hidden Under The Cloak Of Love
By Norbert Gora

I live bathed in the rain
born of the clouds
of overwhelming feeling
in each droplet
lurks a pinch of love

this downpour
dries out all the fear
enriches the lake of my happiness
to the bottom
the risk of flooding does not scare

I would drown
in the blue of your eyes
I could traverse
this sweet azure ocean
to the end of sparking stars
take my hand and hide
under the cloak of love
let its unbreakable structure
protects us
from the storm of bad moments

in spite of envious glances
words that hurt like a knife
we weave a shield with kisses
it separates us
from contempt of hostile faces

Plaza Girl
By Greg Bogaerts

My wife and I visit Melbourne every year for a fortnight. I could only describe my visits there as creating a feeling that I am being nurtured; it is a place, not just of cafes and coffee, but of galleries and bookshops, and trams that rattle through my dreams as I lay sleeping in our flat in St Kilda. It has reached the point where I feel as though we live in Melbourne for two weeks each year, and holiday in Newcastle for the other fifty. Melbourne has become home; Newcastle is a prison, from which we cannot escape, its tawdry grubby skyline, the street violence, the rampart unemployment, the grinding philistinism and the obsession with rugby league, making shackles that hold us securely.

I have come to identify with many of the people, who live in St Kilda, Windsor and Prahahn; they have become more real to me than the people in Newcastle with whom I've lived all of my life.

The little down-syndrome kid, who catches the North Richmond tram every morning, sits opposite us, grinning so hard that I think his mouth will split.

The old lady, who sits out the front of Coles in Chapel Street, propositioning the male check out workers, chews the fat, telling us of her life and loves, before waddling across the road on painful arthritic legs to buy her bottle of port from Dan Murphy's.

The Italian bloke, who owns the small grocery next to the old picture theatre in Chapel Street, makes the best cup of coffee in the city; but he doesn't brag about it, and his customers tell no one, preferring to keep the superb long blacks and café lattés to themselves.

The Yugoslav man, who sees the students of St Michaels across busy Chapel Street, blowing his whistle and waving his big flag to stop the cars, has become a friend. He always stops the traffic for my wife and me to cross, even though we aren't students.

But the person who haunts me is the young Italian woman, who works in the Plaza arcade in Prahran. She's very beautiful with long black hair and wide brown eyes; her skin is white and her smile ready. But it's her capacity for work, and maybe suffering, that are remarkable.

She works six days a week, well into the afternoon and night. Christina, as her father, the owner of the small café, calls her, never stops, pouring coffee, cooking pizzas, ladling pasta into the stainless steel tubs in the display window and scrubbing the kitchen out the back.

Sometimes I wonder whether she has a family, a husband

and children, or whether it's just Christina and her father. Over the years, I've watched her beauty wane and fade because of her punishing work load. I've wondered how to release her from what seems to me little more than slavery, but, then again, it's none of my business.

Still, there are moments in the Plaza that give me a small sliver of hope. That's when Christina seems to slough off her servitude; her beauty seems to flare up, defeating her fate, her eyes flash with defiance, leaving me breathless.

Walter
By John Stockdill

Professor Julian Buchanan hurt his knuckles knocking on the heavy oak door. It was unlocked. He stepped into the room, rubbing one hand with the other.

"Walter, we've got to talk."

Walter was pointing binoculars out the window, beard blowing gently around thick wrists. He remained seated.

"You could spend your life up here, staring out with those things."

"Thanks. I'd like that."

Julian turned a full circle.

"No Walter. Listen, I'm your brother. Jesus Christ…"

"My brother, Jesus Christ. Absurd."

"Stop it, Walt. I'm serious. This arrangement isn't working. You frighten Linda."

The leather elbow of Julian's tweed jacket emitted a feeble squeak as he leaned on the polished dresser. He lit a small cigar. "Oh Walter, pour me a drink. Can't we just start with a fresh attitude? If you could just hold a rational conversation."

Julian stopped. He was staring at a piece of satin material protruding from a drawer. Cigar in teeth, one eye on Walter, he opened it in squeaking increments. A bra. Squeak. A smorgasbord of Linda's lingerie. The cigar dropped from Julian's open mouth. He turned on his heels and fled.

Walter trained his glasses on the figure hurrying from the building, out into the park, until it disappeared under a canopy of fig trees. Slowly Walter stood, stretched, and ambled over to the dresser, picking up the smouldering cigar. His eyes followed the blue smoke that streamed from his nostrils toward the ornate ceiling.

"Linda? You can come out now. He's gone."

Hair
By Bee Parkinson

We always knew that life was going to change,
We were aware of this from quite an early age.
Mum's hair would change regularly, every month or two,
She was like a rainbow, a human rainbow with the smile of stars.

I remember her clearly, as though it were yesterday.
To me it was yesterday, because yesterday isn't always yesterday.
Sometimes yesterday is what we make of it,
For it is simply a day that came before today.

We used to walk the dogs, who grew older and older,
They used to run and jump and her hair was orange.
Then they began to walk slowly and her hair was brown,
Then they limped on tired legs, and her hair was greying,

We used to make fairy cake's together, home recipe.
I used to lick the cake and icing bowls, and her hair was green.
Then the recipe fell to the pre-made box, and her hair was blonde,
Then we bought the pre-baked from the supermarket when her hair was white.

We used to sing and dance with smiles and laughter,
And for so long her hair was brightest blue.
Then we stopped dancing but still we sang, she with black hair.
The singing stopped after a while, and her hair began to fall out.

I remember the days in the library reading to each other,
Oh and her hair was a fantastic purple unlike any I'd ever seen.
Then we read our own books, and I knew she had a dye job,
It wasn't long till her hair was all gone and I read at her bedside.

I remember my mum as though it were yesterday,
For her life was yesterday to me, it was our yesterday.
I still remember our last yesterday, sitting in his hospital room,
Her face pale and drawn against stark white pillow.

I took her hand yesterday because I knew I needed to.
She smiled at me with lips chapped and bleeding.
I told her I loved her, and she said she loved me too,
And she would never forget the dogs, the cakes, the books or the singing.

In my today I'm told she is gone and nothing can change it.
I'm told to move on and that it's an old story, her story.
It's not her story though, it's mine too; it's ours.

I'm on one page see, and she's waiting for me on the other,
And when it's my tomorrow I know it'll be spent with her again,
And we'll be holding hands again, and her hair will be the Rainbow again.

A Romance
By John Karl Stokes

Sunset flares over the mall,
a cosmology of ice-cream;
the divine compromise
takes place in a car-park:

The contraceptive rain
is negotiated,
the deferral of hope
in favour of a chorus of sparrows

is agreed, pending
a resolution
of the school year problem,
dinner

is brought up again.
They part company thump, thump
But will meet again
someday when the music blares.

The Third Woman
By Darren Sharp

The Second Woman To Enter The Independent Coffee Shop Grabbed A Latte And Left.

The third woman to enter the coffee shop was on her phone. Although she physically had a phone to her ear, it proved worthy alibi to avoid awkwardness. Joe knew all the tricks. A hat offered safety barrier to avert eyes; useful aid for fiddling, giving hands in danger of vacant episode occupation attached to sweaty palm. A newspaper gave opportunity to peruse the room, casually, glancing as if in-between paragraphs.

Tall. Alive. Womanly. Most definitely not appearing solitary. Was this her?

Joe glanced down, his *Guardian* was not his usual read, in fact he found the world was an uncomfortable place in black and white print. War, ecological disaster, privileged Royal babies born clutching platinum rattles, happy couples announcing nuptials. Who wanted to know such pain, banality or injustice.

Joe reverted to the third woman. He began to believe her phone conversation was not an alibi. Maybe she was chatting. To someone. Joe was impressed. Then flicking her hair just the right side of vivacious, the heavens opened, tears formed and Joe almost fell off his chair. He was desperate, not blind.

'No way. Seriously?' The third woman laughed, 'Gotta go. Yes, in town. A date.' Laughter gave way to delirium. 'I know, I know'.

Raven36 was mid-thirties and the third woman to enter the coffee shop since Joe arrived. That was all Joe knew. As *Raven36* approached his table, he regretted his ethical stance on pictures, wishing he had sent his beaming smile on top of that camel in Marrakech, confirming his sterling sense of adventure and fun. Sitting atop the camel was higher than expected, so possibly his smile could be perceived as grim determination. Joe needed that now. He was at the dawn of a new era.

'Joe? Is it?'

'Joe. Yes. I'm Joe. Joe by name, Joe by nature. Joe'.

Talking. Empathising. Mirroring body language. Direct eye contact; revolutionary. Smiling, without showing excessive teeth. God she was good at this. Surely *Raven36* met loads of men through her work. Yes she was gainfully employed, as a Social Worker, with contract, annual leave and health benefits. Like in the movies. Joe imagined being referred to talk with her winning smile. On a crumbling cliff edge Joe knew the third woman would talk him down and their bond would be complete. Joe knew it was meant to be. Forever. He preferred a Son. He hoped she preferred a Daughter. Then they would try for two Or four. Joe found odd numbers troubling.

Joe found his head nodded frequently. *Raven36* said she listened a lot at work, but he could not help noticing she had not answered his earlier direct question.

'*Raven36* is a great name for online, what is your.. your real name?'

When not working *Raven36* enjoyed para-gliding, rock climbing, something else that was lost on him and Rosé wine. Joe wondered how she found the time to open a bottle between exclaiming the exhilaration of extreme sports. Perhaps she preferred a wine box on the go? Joe's stomach muscles ached from holding in his gut. A lifetime of pies steadied minds but wobbled extremities.

Their Coffee was exhilarating, so delicious, to the power of ten. An unusual occurrence.

'Joe, you have somewhere we can go?'

Just to be sure he asked her to repeat. Confident and strong.

His suburban mind blew. Was it new house blend?

Now, Joe then knew he was invisible to her. *Raven36* needed anonymous male validation. And that was okay. He'd been brief anonymous distraction. 'Couldn't stop watching your smile even if I tried', said Joe. Like the transition from VHS to DVD, he would never forget the clarity of those thirty minutes.

Now, Joe wished he knew her real name, for he had not pushed. Forever she remained the third woman. And no one could live up to her. The third woman. The only woman.

I Am A Candle
By Dayle Ashton

I am a candle,
Burning brightly
When you enter the room,
Trembling when you
Breathe close to me,
Sending my flickering
Light toward your
Beautiful face
And casting soft images
Of love on the wall,
Until you lay on your bed
Exhausted and spent,
Wrapped in my glow,
Drifting off to blissful sleep.
Later, I see you rise silently,
Closing the door behind you,
Leaving with the morning light,
I don't burn so bright then,
The shadows on the wall
Grow dim, hard to see,
Remaining only as memories
From the nights
When you loved me

A Love Lost
By Megan MacLeod

A moment, a glimpse
A touch, a kiss
Caresses that glitter
Touches that shimmer

A mere moment in time
Both exquisite and true

No more discovered
No more realized

But forever loved

Crash
By Megan Costigan

The joy crashed over her
knocking her backwards into the ocean and sky
and she laughed and cried and danced
under the water with her heart
full and thumping and free and

rose up out of the salted water
in a sparkle of sun and magic and
a tiny bit of love and
after a breath and a shiver
cried out to the empty beach

come dance with me
in my deep green ocean
of hope and starfish
stretching pink
into my heart

dance with me
under and now above
the cresting green waves
in a crash of joy

Roman Love
By Jo Wilson-Ridley

Remembering June, 1994.

On his first morning in Rome -
his first morning in any overseas
country, my lover flung open the
kitchen shutters exposing his naked
body to the unsuspecting courtyard

'Ciao Roma' he hollered. Milling pigeons
should've squawked and scattered
as slack washing lines snapped taut -
but it was my earth trembling
as the white sky blended

Turning to study the Italian percolator
his face hijacked by a curious grin
my heart swelled. Yes - I will elope
to Florence with this man, unreservedly
embracing the chariots only Rome can offer

Sunset
By Brian Langley

Sunset - Clouds on fire
Hover on an oily sea
Waves wash gently on the sand
And you are here with me

We walk along the water's edge
Where land and sea unite
Where pools of water in the rocks
Reflect the evening light.

And hand in hand together
But in our separate ways
We walk toward the sunset
Of the evening of our days

Previously published 2012 in *You Could Write a Poem About That*.

Our Billy
By John Stockdill

A monster lived down the lane, that's what they said. After school, my little sister and I peered through the narrow aperture of fence palings, and there he was. Bouncing slowly toward us, like an elephant on the ocean floor, he hung over a canvas sling tethered to a Hills Hoist Clothesline.

A gas mask swung before his bandaged face, straps pushing pink ears forward. His bagpipe breathing providing little harmonic twists to the rhythm of the squeaking hoist. To this music he danced a circle, arms outstretched in a strangely elegant arc. He seemed to be conducting the white billowing sheets pegged just beyond his reach, like vanishing sails on his horizon. As he bounced past our faces, two medals pinned to his pyjama shirt would glint in the afternoon sun. We were totally entranced, too aghast to look away. If only we had.

"Hello there, girls. It's alright, our Billy wouldn't hurt a fly."

We jumped up, straightened our tunics, and bolted down toward the Harbour. Breathless, we settled on a sandstone wall. Legs dangling, we gazed out toward Sydney Heads, all those big ships going about their mysterious business. My little sister began sniffling, donating her tears and snot to the rising tide.

"That poor Billy. He's not a monster. What happened?"

"I don't know Sis. I suppose they sent him out on one of those big ships, and he came back home on another."

"No. He's trying to come back home, but he just goes around and around."

"It's alright though Sis, it's alright, because that lady really loves him."

Love On High
By David Watt

I saw her once and 'twas enough to kindle passion's flame
From tinder of unrealised dreams;
Her beauty was to blame,
For sparking a desire in me from middle to the seams.

Each day I frequented the place on High Street where we met
In hope of meeting up again on pretext or excuse,
And striking conversation 'bout her hair or better yet,
Cafes we could rendezvous. But tell me, what's the use?

For she wasn't there on Monday, or Tuesday, or the rest
Of days when I was ready to suitably impress.
My lines were planned, new shirt well-pressed,
But nothing did I see, of gracefulness personified in floral summer dress.

I asked around the neighbourhood for clues to whereabouts,
A hint of her employment, or name to match her face.
The lack of information I obtained led but to doubts,
For a girl of her description couldn't vanish without trace!

In daydreams born of longing, though fantasies of youth
Minds are prone to wander to remedy such ills,
Relishing the prospect, certain in the truth
That love resides in High Street, if imagination wills.

The Going From The Valley
By John Karl Stokes

No more. No other. A kind
of living saw us in:
a swelling in of seasons
years saying nothing
touches while a hand thickened
and another's thinned.

There was one hope – the last
that we'd live on
in memory of one another
each breath along the path
a caress, each cry of our children
a celebration.

But what, in the end, can anyone say
about a life? ... only this:
that we stuck it out
out of sheer, blind, stupid love
and at an end, could say
Goodbye *Goodbye.*

Published in magazines c.2000 – 2005.

From Your Loving Daughter
By Karishma Krishna Kumar

Friday, 12th March
1993, Bombay

Dear Ma,

It's almost as if flashcards; the ones that we'd give to the children in kindergarten for their ABCs; yeah, flashcards like those.
 That's what this past decade has felt like to me. There are so many unopened boxes in my past, that my expanding mind is quickly filling up.
 Like a loop, my mind goes back and forth; in and out, and sometimes walking through the dark alleyways of the past, I am actually, in fact, sitting in the present.
 Ma, I am sorry. I know that I've been all over the place. And, maybe, still am. I wake up bang in the middle of an ongoing conflict and don't realise that I am the one who started the riot. Ma, I am, really, really sorry.
 Ma, with you and me, it's different. We're both volatile, combustible even. When you or I get upset, we kick and scream and let go. That's it Ma. We. Let. Go.
 And so, it's okay the next day to talk about *kadi-chawal*. Or the maid. Or the telephone bill. But it's not the same with Pa. You should have told me, Ma. Because, I guess, perhaps, only you knew! Because Ma, truly, only you know Pa well enough to know.
 Ma, I am sorry that I told you my secret. It is a burden you didn't deserve to carry; for the rest of your life. But. Ma.
 Ma, I got scared. These nightmares began roughly fifteen years ago and then those nightmares started becoming real. Ma.
 Ma. Ma, I am sorry. I couldn't tell reality apart from the dream. Ma. Ma. I'm sorry.
 I got confused. But, I tried Ma. I did. To thwart the itch under my foot, the dry roof of my mouth. I tried, Ma, to trust.
I forced myself back into the reality that was almost similar to the nightmare, Ma. I'm sorry. The thwarting didn't work Ma. It just didn't.
 I'm afraid of intimacy now; now that the nightmares are more real than reality to me, Ma. I want to run. Ma. I want to change this awful reality that doesn't need to be mine; anymore. I want a second chance, Ma.
 A do-over? I want another shot at living again, learning again.
 Finding myself and I don't know Ma, maybe. Maybe. Try

falling in love again? I don't know Ma.

The possibilities are endless. So many billions of things; that are nothing like the things that you, me and Pa saw. Nothing like that at all.

Ma, maybe there's love on the other side. Ma. Maybe in that reality; across that bridge Ma; you, me and Pa; don't fight anymore. Maybe?

I love you, Ma.

Thank you for never ever ever leaving my side, Ma. And Ma, thank you for Pa.

Love,

Your daughter
PS. *I made custard. It's in the fridge.*

Til Death Us Do Part
By Jenna Rainey

The summer haze that often fills the evenings has given way to a gale of howling wind and streaming rain, which washes the windows clean of any streak or smear brought about by the aging fields that surround us. Adrian has popped out to provided food for the three of us and it's him I think of out in the thunderous brut of an evening as I lounge in-front of the flickering hearth, listening to the force of the storm protruding against our stone-walled inhabitance. I pass away an hour with my thoughts alone, reading an absconded activity with the sheer volume of the gale outside.

There's a rattling of the door, heralding my future husband's return. He comes baring bags filled with old news wrappers, which can only mean one thing. Fish n' chips for tea, with mushy peas and a milky brew to wash it down with. How I crave for a small alcoholic measurement, but the little one won't allow it, branded an unnecessary risk. We tuck in in a civilized manner at our small oak table and talk of the weather and, but only briefly, touch on any sentiment of work. The topic lasts merely moments, when the little electricity we have cuts out and Ade gets up to fetch the matches and substitute resources. Instinctively I rest a hand over my stomach, caressing it. A reassuring gesture to the unborn foetus inside.

I jump suddenly, as complete darkness curtains my sight, but feel a familiar touch fall upon my shoulder. He aids me up, no peeking he says, as he leads me blindly from room to room.

I hear a door close as he parts his grasp. I re-adjust my eyes after he signals I should open them.

And you've brought me to the boudoir because?
Well the lights are out...

He set the lantern on the bedside locker and ruefully approached. Withdrawing the already dishevelled cardigan from my shoulders he led me to the bed where I was seated and in a sultry manner he slowly unwoven the buttons from his shirt. There is something to be said for revealing your vulnerable nature to another under such pressing circumstance as amongst the threatening world outside. Lying there barely clothed, storm shadows dancing about my skin, hairs stand on end at his touch. The wind whistles through the weaves, whips under the doors, creates a draft that makes me shiver.

He loves me, he loves me, he loves me not, he loves me...
I remind myself.

Our intimacy is electric but intimidating at times. I have to ensure he doesn't hurt the baby, its innocence my priority above all. I question why we really came here, to this ramshackle cottage amongst this god-forsaken land and I remind myself that I made a vow when I engaged myself that night. I glance to the bronzed ring upon my finger and admit my own demise. I was too naïve and cultivated to step backward from my journey into the realms of an exceedingly shadier future.

I awaken to the sound of the birds the next morning, their chirping calls echoing across the open fields. The light is soft and glowing, like heaven decent after the passing storm. I lie cushioned between his body and the covers I've stolen to my side of the bed. Cocooned in the scent of the new dawn around me, as if I could escape the intrusion of the other nature I see embedded in him. Never mind, more fool me, this is my present, gateway to my future, this is what I took to be mine and so it is; til death us do part.

Lust-Less Love
By Kariuki wa Nyamu

Darling
My love for you is the boundless Indian Ocean
Yeah! One which is meant to last
forever without lust
and if I may tell you
since I dreamt of you last night
my heart has been full
and it's doorway wide open
for you, my one and only
who's young and beautiful like the rainbow!

Listen
My love for you is the dew
on the fresh green flora in early morning
where no one can re-kindle
our never-dying love
and if I may let you know
Your love is the sweetest gift ever
for without it, our lust-less love
nothing good would happen in life!

Oh! My darling
I see you looking at me and smile
So, why don't you come to me, for I love you dear
and I want to make you feel beautiful
just be kind a while
though still coy of your newly sprang twin towers
quite intact like wild oranges
give me an intimate hug
for that's what we should proclaim
intimate love!
Oh! Come on sweet, just give me a dry kiss
if nothing else!
For we need each other desperately
to ensure our happiness.

Last Goodbye
By Angharad Thompson Rees

I could not bear the moment to witness his last breath,
The tragic love story ended there beside me his death,
His spirit gone, my soul destroyed and broken is my heart,
As if my life has no meaning, now that we're apart.

Although I don't feel it, my heart still beats but hollow like a drum,
My once bright spirit broken now as soulless I become,
In my darkest hour, I screamed and cursed up at the moon,
That the love I lost so fresh and new was taken all too soon.

But then I heard him call me, in the silence of my dream,
I felt his presence alive as if next to me it would seem,
His soul became transparent, right through him I could see,
As he calmed my restless spirit and he softly spoke to me.

He whispered "My fair lady, I'll always be close by,
I'm every star that's shining in the heavens of the sky,
I'm with you every day as braking dawn has began,
And lay sweet kisses on your skin as it is warmed up by the sun.

When the gentle breeze blows through your hair, believe me this is true,
You'll hear my voice call your name and whisper 'I love you',
And when the summer rain falls upon your skin so fair,
These raindrops are my tears of love, reminding you I am there.

I am the golden leaves in autumn that fall down on your lawn,
I am the morning chorus of birds singing that it is dawn,
And when the waves are crashing and sun shines on the sea,
The golden shimmer on the water, darling that is me.

You'll always have me near you, just listen to nature's call,
I'll kiss your face so softly now as snow begins to fall,
And seeing you fall in love again, the best gift that would be,
As falling in love brings you alive, a gift from you to me.

So now you know that I surround you every second of the day,
And every night I'll be beside you whilst in your bed you lay,
I'm with you always my special love, always by your side,
Because in your heart, forever yours, that's where I reside."

The Last Bye
By Nikita Krishna Kumar

I don't know when I sleep off. The really deep sleep. I never know. The one that transports you into the parallel universe.

I wake up this morning and I am already preparing myself to "miss" him. He is leaving. To catch his dreams. The ones he had before I met him. That is one of the most important things, I believe. Having dreams regardless of the other person. Moulding each other's dreams to become the best version of the idea.

I get up and decide to make my cup of tea. There's a little family discussion happening. I walk in completely caught unaware. I am not a morning person. Not. At. All. A conversation with me is like talking to a wall. I'm listening to you when you talk. But I don't remember or respond in the right way. I normally get really loud in the morning if spoken to. I like gathering my mind and its multiple thoughts. So when I was asked a question which I had a genuine answer for - I screeched.

All this while, him leaving lingered on my mind. I knew what I needed. A massage and some sister bonding. I was comfortable in the zone. Dad was going back too. Gloomy day. I don't like goodbyes. They mess with your head. They confuse you more than necessary.

He texted! He was back for the night. He leaves tomorrow.

Guess the last bye doesn't really have to be when you think he is back. For the night. The thought is comforting. It's still only a few extra hours. I won't be getting all those extra hours.

I get ready to see him one last time before he leaves. And I am actually thinking about what to wear. Which side do I surprise him with? What look has he not yet seen? How beautiful can I look for him?

I know for a fact that we'll talk. Which is so much fun. He is the second most interesting person I've met. I think I'm the most interesting person. So anyone can imagine the interesting conversations we have. He's my friend. He's my fun place. He appreciates me. He feels my emotions. My pain. Tries everything to make me smile. Notices every breath I take, move I make. He has conversations with himself imagining me, which he would never admit to doing.

So I guess the Last Bye, isn't going to become *The Last Goodbye*. At least not now.

After Love
By Pamela Scott

I tell you I love you
and turn the world upside down.
You whisper the same words
in my ear and make my heart leap.

You fall silent, unable to look at me
and unsure of what you feel.
It all changed after I said the L word.
Our love isn't the same after my heart finds a voice.

You act so strange sometimes, avoid spending
time with me and push me away.
Awkwardness drives a wedge between us.
We'd been so close before those three damn words.

You stop answering my text messages
or returning my telephone calls.
You cancel plans at the last minute.
You're too busy to see me, talk to me or spend time with me.

Coldness replaces our once red-hot passion
and the big freeze makes the wedge even wider.
You say you feel the same, whisper those words in my ear
in a moment of passion - so why do you push me away?

I try to talk to you about what it means
to the both of us, but you're always too busy.
All I want to do is hold you, but you
avoid even hearing my voice on the phone.

Conversations used to flow like a river
dry up and turn into a puddle.
We used to talk and laugh for hours
now we struggle to fill large silences.

The flutter of excitement in my stomach
is replaced by a dull ache of fear.
The goodnight texts starts to fade out
and the weekly night outs stop completely.

My bed's cold without your and my heart breaks.

My arms are empty and my lips miss your taste.
You don't say how much you miss me
and want me every day. I don't exist anymore.

I want to take those three little words back,
make it like it was before but I'm too late.
I open the door to my secret heart.
Nothing is as it was after love.

Do You Think Of Me?
By Zondrae King

At dawn, when all the waving beds of meadow grasses bow their heads
release their heavy burden of the dew,
do morning dreams transport you back to times when we were one?
The days were long and warm but they were few.

And when the gentle warmth of day has wiped the tears of dew away
and lofty spears of green salute the sun,
do you recall the hours we lay there, looking at the sky,
just counting cloudy patterns one by one?

At noon, when even birds seek shade, from blazing sun in leafy glade
while endless heat is falling on the earth,
do you think twice of idle days we sat beside the lake?
We counted not the cost but more the worth.

Our fingers made a lovers knot as time and trouble, we forgot.
No sound could break the magic of the day.
We found the only world we wanted in each others eyes
not needing words to chase the peace away.

Then when the gentle evening brings a momentary pause that sings,
a melody of unfragmented still,
do you find sometimes that you halt, recalling distant nights,
when I would follow, gladly, at your will?

And do you stop to find the hush concealed beyond the work days rush
and search for me within the madding crowd.
Then catch a glimpse that could be me, prepare with silent breath to see,
if now you need to call my name aloud.

Do you still look for me in dreams, and find me, with a smile that seems
to linger, near the place where we first met?
Then give my hand a tender kiss and walk a while with me,
surrender without thought, without regret.

Has this world roughly torn apart, your soul so sweet, your gentle heart

and crushed from you the spark that I loved so?
Or do you ponder, musing on what really might have been,
if fate had been our friend and not our foe?

When you upon your death bed lie, so pale and still, and yet you try
to wander through the pages of your life,
will memories you dwell upon be times I shared with you?
We knew our love could only bring us strife.

Then will you look with vision clear and hope once more to see me near
and wonder did I often think of you?
And as the end approaches, dear, will I stretch out my hand,
to whisper long forbidden vows, "I do".

Too Broken To Bend
By Karishma Krishna Kumar

it all started one day over tea,

and then she said to him,
it is all pretty clear, you see,
life is just another fantasy.
we all do what we want on just another whim.

seasons change from time to time,
it is winter today and summer comes in tomorrow.
you would be sensible to hold onto to your last dime,
because then it will be the rainy day filling you with sorrow.

well, if you must know,
all this talk about love is merely nothing,
love is just another puppet show,
everything in it hangs by the thinnest string.

I have eyes that see another day come to life,
but, then I close them and pretend that this night will never end.
I think of all the hurt, pain and strife,
believing that I am too broken to bend.

I think I am just too broken to bend.

Sometimes
By Molly Donald

Sometimes I do not want someone to tell me everything is okay.

There are times I want, or need, to be told the truth
and maybe it is best to come from you.
Turning myself into a corpse, decaying from the inside out,
minute by minute, the clock
a persistent parental knock.
Ticking in the back of my head to remind me that I am a bomb
waiting to explode.
I apologise for my convenience, I just need to be held close.

I am sorry for being so clingy
whilst often so detached from the world around me.
As though I am a lone planet orbiting around the Earth myself.
It gets lonely with all this space, yet I
cling to you with feline grace
that I cannot stop or let you escape.

Sometimes I need to be lied to - be convinced everything is okay.

I primarily need to be fed lies from you,
kissed until my red mixes with your blue -
and we become a purple mess,
just a bundle of cells undressed.
Give me anything. Let lies spill from your lips like salt water
overflows from these lids.

A wreck in the sea;
the destruction of such an untouchable masterpiece.
Fingertips as gentle as can be
do not let me escape from my blissful dream
just let me ignore reality.

The End
By Barbara Hawthorn

moving out moving on
he did help with the boxes
- books being so heavy -
two staircases down
but it was all so bland
no tight lips   no shouting
nobody cried
there should have be tears surely?

hard to say who was being dumped...
we should have bickered?
who gets to keep
-those CDs we bought together?
there was sweetness in those years
wasn't there?
then he dumped in my duffel bag
closed the boot
with quite unnecessary force
I started the engine
"See you around" he said
smacked his open hand on the roof –
was that if not an olive branch
at least a twig?

in the rear mirror
he looked so forlorn
watching in the road
that I drove around the block –
but he was gone when I returned
the door was shut like a snub.

Contributors...

Akwu Sunday Victor
Akwu was born 1987, hails from Etutekpe, Olamaboro L.G.A. Kogi State, Nigeria. He holds a degree in English and Literary Studies from Kogi State University, Anyigba and is presently a postgraduate student of Literature. He is a poet and critic. His critical papers have appeared in scholarly journals in Nigeria and abroad.
E: akwueneojo@yahoo.com

Alan Murphy
Alan is the Irish writer and illustrator of three collections of poetry for young readers. Dublin-born, he currently lives in Lismore, county Waterford. His latest collection, *Prometheus Unplugged*, was listed in a children's and young adults' books of the year article in the *Irish Times*. He has been featured in children's poetry anthologies in the UK and America. "A lot of incredible talent has emerged recently from Ireland. Alan Murphy is one of the them." - Anastasia Gonis, *Buzz Words* magazine.
E: alanmu@eircom.net
W: Avantcardpublications.com

Alasdair S. Goudie
Alasdair is a Scottish-based English writer, currently studying Creative Writing at undergrad level. His work flitters between several projects, some novels/novellas, some plays, and none of them really complete yet. He writes poetry in his spare time, and finds referring to himself in the third person whilst writing bios rather weird. He can be found by typing 'Alasdair Goudie' into most internet places, because nobody else has a name that specifically odd. Find him on Upwork or Fiverr to provide his hypothetical children with sustenance.
E: aligoudie@hotmail.com

Andrew Hunter
"I live and write in Glasgow and have had work published in *Envoi* and *Northwords Now*. The Poetry Scotland website *The Open Mouse*, run by the poet Colin Wills, has also taken my work, and I've had non-fiction work taken by magazines."
E: swimminghome@hotmail.co.uk

Angharad Thompson Rees
Angharad is a Sydney Based travel and lifestyle writer and spoken word poet. Originally from Wales, her wanderlust has seen her travelling the globe to discover the world's oceans and emotions. A

keen surfer and once professional horsewoman, Angharad now resides in the Northern Beaches, embarking on new journey as a children's author, and is currently awaiting the release of her fantasy novel-in-verse for children, *The Making of a Knight*.
E: amrees.contact@gmail.com
W: www.angharadthompsonrees.com

Barbara Hawthorn
Barbara lives in Auckland, New Zealand. She is a retired teacher (Mathematics) with a lifelong addiction to writing. Currently a member of International Writers' Workshop, Northcote, New Zealand, Barbara is a musician, playing mandola in The Auckland Mandolinata Orchestra.
E: john.hawthorn@xtra.co.nz

Bee Parkinson
"I am british based in Scotland, and a writer of poetry, short stories, novels and plays. My published work includes a short story in a Scholastics book published in my high school, a poem on the back of the Fife Children's Rights Strategy Document. I also co-wrote the first two issues of a comic book series published by Devolution Comics and one on my poems is part of a Kickstarter for an anthology titled *The Chronicles of Ollundra*. I enjoy writing, travelling, theatre and cosplaying and charity work."
E: jokingcupid@gmail.com

Bernadette Perez
Bernadette is a poet possessing expression and creativity. In 1990 she received the Silver Poet Award from World of Poetry. Her work has appeared in *The Wishing Well; Musings* in 2010, *Small Canyons Anthology* in 2013, *Poems 4 Peace* in 2014. *Fix and Free Anthology* in 2015. She is the Vice President of the New Mexico State Poetry Society and member of Rio Grande Valencia Poets since 2005.
E: bpburritos@aol.com

Brian Langley
"I live in suburban Perth, the capital of Western Australia with my wife of fifty plus years. I write Bush Poetry, Australian rhyming poetry which has near perfect metre and consistency of structure. I write across many subjects and perform (mostly from memory) regularly at retirement villages, aged care facilities, country festivals, service and social clubs etc., etc. I perform under the name *The City Poet* - this is due to me being a member of the Western Australian Bush Poets Association, many members of which have a rural background and write on rural subjects - most of my poetry is from the point of

view of an Australian city dweller. My poems reflect my lifestyle, age and interests, mainly ageing, being Australian, the environment, travelling, fishing and contemporary living. I also delve occasionally into politics and history. I have self published several books as well as some audio CDs and a couple of e-books of historic Western Australian poetry. I was born in rural Western Australia but came to the city in my teens. Following a career in telecommunications, I retired and started writing a family history. I found that I had a poet (Leigh Hunt) in my ancestry and looked up his work. I was far from impressed and thought I could do better, so I commenced writing, mostly contemplative short poems. - that was back in the mid 1990s. Since then my poetry has changed direction somewhat, now being mostly classified as Australian Bush Poetry.
E: briandot@tpg.com.au
W: Brianlangley.wabushpoets.asn.au

Brigette Furlonger
Writer and photographer Brigette, has enjoyed creating for as long as she can remember. Her love of writing has blossomed over the past 10 years. As a mother, wife, sister, traveller and a nature lover, Brigette has new material to explore at her fingertips. Also, she feels her writing and photography are symbiotic, and encourage new creations everyday. It has only been recently that she has become more public with her work. Over the last few years, Brigette's photography and writing have been in several shows and books. Her accomplishments include winning the People's Choice Award for a short story submitted to the Duncan Journal, being short-listed for a nationwide poetry competition, and being one of the contributors and photographers for *Word and Vision*.
E: bcfurlonger@gmail.com
Blog: Saanichinletphotosblog.wordpress.com

Carol Ann
Carol Ann was born in S.E. London in 1948 and is now a grandmother in her sixties. She has lived in the foothills of the Grampian Mountains for the last 19 years and after a lifetime working in the IT industry has 'retired' to indulge her passions for travel, writing and photography. These travels have provided an abundant supply of source material for her writing and she is particularly interested in exploring the links between sacred landscapes, their legends and underlying geology. As a member of Huntly Writers, Carol has been involved in various poetry readings and performances and contributed to recent anthologies including *Weaving Words* and the soon to be published paranormal anthology *Open With Care*. She has also published a children's book called *Rifka, the Adventures of a*

Gnome.

Cath Bore
Cath is a writer of fiction and fact from Merseyside, UK. Her flash fiction can be found, amongst other places, in *National Flash Fiction Day* anthologies 2014 and 2015. Non-fiction wise, she writes about feminism, books, lifestyle and music for a number of publications. Cath is a panelist for Bay TV's *52%* programme, broadcast across Merseyside, Cheshire – and Birmingham. She has an MA in Creative Writing from Liverpool John Moores University. She co-wrote the screenplay for the feature film *Big Society – The Musical* (2013). Cath is currently completing a crime novel.
E: cathbore@googlemail.com
Blog: Cathbore.wordpress.com
Twitter: @cathbore

Catherine Morgans
Catherine has always had a creative slant but it's only recently that she's chosen to explore writing for fun as an outlet for her artistic expression. While dabbling in a number of writing projects she has ignited a long past passion for poetry.
E: morganscatherine@gmail.com

Chris Kempling
Chris is a retired teacher/counsellor from Kamloops, British Columbia, Canada. He is in complete agreement with Nobel Prize winning poet Joseph Brodsky, who said; "Poetry is perhaps the only insurance we've got against the vulgarity of the human heart." Chris is married with three adult children, and five 'amazing' grandchildren. He writes a regular religion column for the local paper (*Kamloops This Week*), and enjoys coin collecting, motorcycling, making Quidditch brooms, and attending vintage car events in his 1976 Lincoln Continental Mark IV.
E: chriskempling@shaw.ca

Clement Clark
Clement was born in a town named Dundee on the northern part of what is today known as Kwa-Zulu-Natal, South Africa. He graduated from Dundee Secondary School in 1994 then worked in numerous companies as a call centre operator. Although he writes both poetry and fiction novels none have been published yet. He currently resides with his wife in Volkrust Mpumalanga province, where he does upholstery.
E: tynnestyle@gmail.com

Clare Lightfoot
E: clarelightfoot2012@gmail.com

Courtney Speedy
Courtney is a 19 year old poet from Whangarei, New Zealand. She has had her poetry published in three separate collections; *Re-Draft: The Word Is Out* (2014), *Write Off Line: They Came in From the Dark* (2014) and *LONELY - A Collection of Poetry and Prose on Loneliness and Being Alone*. Her inspiration comes from the world around her and music in particular. She is working towards self-publishing a collection of her poetry and prose in the near future.
E: courtneyleoniejayne@gmail.com

Darren Sharp
"I am British, based in UK. My writers' bio: October 2014 Omnibus, Claphan - a pop-up play written as a commission, performed as part of Omnibus, Clapham's 125 anniversary event, directed by Scott Le Crass. Summer 2015, New Vic Theatre, Hoard Festival - monologue part of New Vic Theatre's, Newcastle-under-Lyme, Staffordshire, after winning their playwriting competition in conjunction with the National Theatre Studio."
E: Dgsharp_Uk@yahoo.com
Twitter: @dsharp73

David Hollywood
David is from Ireland and and married with four children. His particular interest is in developing a public enthusiasm for poetry among those who aspire but to, but haven't yet made the leap into proclaiming their verse. As a result, he founded and for four years directed The Colours of Life poetry festival's in Bahrain, and latterly is working upon doing the same in Antigua before bringing it to Waterford upon his return. He is the author of an eclectic collection of poems titled *Waiting Spaces* plus contributed to *My Beautiful Bahrain, Poetic Bahrain, More of My Beautiful Bahrain*, and *LONELY – A Collection of Poetry and Prose on Loneliness and Being Alone*. David is also the in-house poet for *Bahrain Confidential* magazine and, as a result, he is one of the most widely read poets in The Middle East. He is also a regular literary critic for *Taj Mahal Review* plus an essayist on the subject of poetry appreciation.There are plans for a new collection of poetry and essays to be released in 2017.
E: davidhollywood23@hotmail.com

David Watt
David is a Canberra, Australia – based writer with a love of creating original and mostly humorous poems and stories. His children's poem

entitled The Clutterbucks received a highly commended award as judged by a panel of primary school children for the 2015 CJ Denis Poetry Competition in Toolangi, Victoria. In his employment with IP Australia, David works with fresh ideas each day. Similarly, his aim in writing is to seek out and create novel approaches and fresh perspectives. He will shortly receive a certificate of commendation for his poem *Shades of Mollymook* in the 2016 Henry Lawson Society Literary Awards.
E: maridav@wattfor.net

Dayle Ashton
"I was born in the Blue Mountains, Australia in 1996. My family moved around New South Wales while I was growing up but I now live near Canberra where I am studying creative writing. I spent my teenage years writing poetry and fiction and have published two collections of poetry including *Forever and Always* (2013) and *From a Café Window* (2015). *Molly's Dreams* is my first novel and I am currently working on two others while trying to get it published. I have a strong sense of social justice and hope that infiltrates my writing, particularly human rights and feminist issues which I feel very strongly about."
E: trublu17@live.com.au

Dominique Megane Clinckemaille
"I have written poetry from an early age as a way of elaborating my world through words. However, my work has had little to no viewers but now, at the age of sixteen, I hope to give my world an audience. I am South African, currently situated the little town of Howick in Kwazulu-Natal. Although born and raised in South Africa, I am of Belgian blood, on my mother's side. On my father's side I am of Brazilian blood."
E: clinckemaillied@gmail.com

Don Adams
Don was in the education field for forty years until an accident prompted his retirement, when he then turned to writing. He has participated in various poetry and short story competitions with some success, and featured a few times in the Award Winning Australian Writers annual publication.
E: theldon@paradise.net.nz

Ella Edwards
"I am sixty-six years of age I began writing bush poetry when I was sixty. I knew nothing about writing or reciting poetry when I joined,I have found the group very supportive. I really enjoy listening to and

reading Australian bush poetry. I was born in England, I have lived in Australia since I was a child. I belong to the Illawarra Breakfast poets group, based in Wollongong, we meet once a week and write a poem every week, sometimes these poems expand into award winning poetry and some have been printed. The group also performs at various venues including aged resident care, rotary meetings and many competitions."
E: ellaedwards@yahoo.com

Elspeth Glenday
"I started writing poetry only after the age of sixty, which was not long ago. Still working part time, I attended an evening class for creative writing. I enjoyed this and, for one of the assignments, I decided to submit some poems. The teacher at the class said he enjoyed reading them and asked me if I enjoyed writing them, which I did. I began to write more and the teacher encouraged me to pursue this,"
E: elspethglenday@yahoo.co.uk

Farha A. Jaleel
"I was born and brought up in Bahrain. I currently live in Sri Lanka. I started out writing short stories at the age of eight and have been passionate about it ever since. I started writing poems a few years ago. I have had one of my short stories published in a local newspaper in Sri Lanka, and some of my poetry in LONELY - A Collection of Poetry and Prose on Loneliness and Being Alone, and hope to get more of my work published in the future."
E: crimson_rose97@yahoo.com

Frank Cardiff
E: cardiff@hotkey.net.au

Frank Meintjies
Frank is based in Johannesburg and works in non-governmental organisations, His poetry has been featured in various journals and he frequently participates in public readings. He also appeared in the book Twelve + One: Some Jo'burg Poets, Their Artistic Lives and Poetry.

Greg Bogaerts
Greg is a writer who lives in Buttaba, Australia. He has had five books of fiction and more than 350 stories published. He is married to Jill and once had a cat called Whisper.
E: gregbogaerts54@gmail.com

Guy Morris
Guy was born in Yorkshire 1962 and, after a multitude of jobs since leaving school, he has worked in transport for the past thirty years, carrying both passengers and heavy goods far and wide. During his travels, seeing all kinds of things to do with life which he likes to put into poems.

Heidi Al Khajah
Heidi is a talented, results-producing publishing and marketing professional with over 15 years experience in her field, with a BA in Publishing. Her career includes publishing, graphic design, marketing and corporate communications, working in the fields of telecom, advertising, aviation and real estate. She recently contributed to the editing team of *The Torch Principle,* and contributed to *LONELY - A Collection of Poetry and Prose on Loneliness and Being Alone.*
E: layle@mail.com
LinkedIn: Bh.linkedin.com/pub/heidi-al-khajah/3/669/b25

Helen Bowers
"I am now retired but words as a journalist, including as inaugural editor of a monthly legal newsletter-cum-magazine. I am a member of the writing group Westerlies. My poetry and short stories have been published in various collections and one of my short stories, *Poet's Corner* won national competition.
E: bowers.helen@gmail.com

Hunter Armstrong
"I am Australian and live in Wagga Wagga NSW Australia. Now that I have retired from the practice of medicine I am concentrating on my writing, in particular short fiction, although I have one or two longer pieces in the pipeline. I have had one short story published and have submitted several more. Some time ago I wrote and published a history of a community choir to which I belonged. I am particularly interested in exploring the various interactions between men and women from the viewpoint of romance and its pitfalls. I use medical scenarios as backdrop. My personal experience allows me to draw on my knowledge for this."
E: s.brucedale.124@bigpond.com

Jacky Perez
Jacky is an American writer, blogger, and traveller. She grew up as an avid reader, writing several short stories in fiction and fantasy in her spare time. After completing a Bachelor of Arts in English, she taught high school English for over seven years in the state of Texas and internationally in South Korea. While she was a teacher, she

published several book reviews and research-based articles for a website that is no longer in business (*Suite101*). While completing a Post-Baccalaureate Certificate in Writing, she discovered her passion for writing creative non-fiction. Currently living in California, she is working towards completing and publishing a memoir about her experiences as an expatriate in South Korea.
E: euo618@gmail.com
W: Jackysjourney.com

James Scalise
Jim is enjoying a life's goal in retirement of writing full time. Architecture, teaching and lecturing have taken him across the US, and through the Middle East to train their architects, engineers and teachers. His published works include numerous presentations and books on the art of teaching, a lengthy essay on Bahrain architecture in *My Beautiful Bahrain*, and the poem *A Conversation in Bahrain* in *My Poetic Bahrain,* and contributed to *LONELY - A Collection of Poetry and Prose on Loneliness and Being Alone.* Jim is an active member of the Writers' League of Texas and the Society of Children's Book Writers and Illustrators.
E: Jim.Scalise@gmail.com

Jenna Rainey
Jenna is a freelance writer, who has a varied backlist of literary credits; in the form of poetry, short-story, interviews and non-fiction; both online and in-print. Having just completed her undergraduate degree in creative writing and publishing, she is currently enjoying writing of her own accord again. Jenna has been engaged in publishing workshops for children, encouraging them to Make A Book at festivals i.e, Forest of Imagination, and is looking forward to assisting with the Bath Children's Literature Festival for the second year in a row this coming Autumn. She is hoping to pursue her masters' degree in creative writing whilst pursuing her ambitions to work in the literary industry.
E: jennaroserainey@yahoo.co.uk

Jennifer Riggs
Jennifer was born in Tanzania, childhood in wartime England, girlhood in Zanzibar, married life in Kenya (in the thick of Mau Mau terrorism), and now in Australia, her writing experiences include: editorial (scientific); contributions to national and international conferences and journals (educational); reviewing (Fiction Focus); broadcasts (ABC Radio National) a novel *The Late Mr Collins* and an anthology for the bereaved *A Handful of Lilies*. Also devising and hosting writers' workshops and the perennial pleasure of just writing, including poetry

– but who wants poetry? Thank goodness you do!
E: riggsclues@bigpond.com

Jessica L. Jackson
Jessica has published four novellas, eight novels of over 100,000 words each, and a collection of short stories as Jessica Lund. She enjoys writing in a variety of romance sub-genres. "There are no genres out there that cannot be turned into a romance. That is what I like best about writing them. The world, as they say, is our oyster. And the pearl is the romantic core." Jessica, mother of three, lives in Southern Alberta with her English husband and two cats.
E: jleolaj1962@gmail.com
W: www.jessicajackson.com

Joe Gallagher
"My name is Joe Gallagher and I am a new writer based in Edinburgh. Last year I spent time living on the streets and wrote several articles for the *Big Issue* about my experiences, under the pseudonym James Campbell, which they published. Subsequently I was nominated for Scottish Features writer of the year Award. I didn't win, but needless to say it was an honour to be considered after a first time effort. I since have spent my time writing short stories and working."
E: jocait1@hotmail.com

John Karl Stokes
John operates out of Canberra, Australia and is internationally known as one of Australia's most courageous and innovative authors, poets and librettists. He has won, been shortlisted, commended, or long-listed for many international prizes, including the Blake, Newcastle, the University of Canberra Vice-Chancellor's International Poetry and the Montreal International Poetry Prizes. He has tutored in poetry and essay-writing; and is a Member and former Board Member of several writers' organisations. At the time of writing his latest full-length collection is Fire in the Afternoon (Halstead Press, 2014). John continues to 'push the boundaries'; He reads his work at international festivals and is in the middle of a passionate campaign to bring back plain-speaking to writings in English.
E: johnstokespoet@me.com
Website: www.johnkarlstokes.com

John R. Sabine
John is into his third career: first a scientist and academic, then a consultant/entrepreneur and now a Scholar-at-Large (thinker, writer, speaker, actor). His recent publications include a major travel memoir and two collections of poetry, as well as several short stories and

essays. A collection of short stories is in press. His acting activities include stage, film and television work – and especially in his stage persona *Old Jack: the Aussie Gleeman* (purveyor of tall tales, short stories and pithy poetry).
E: jsabine@iimetro.com.au
W: www.jsabine.com

John Stockdill
John worked for many years as a musician, and studied visual arts at the Australian National University. He has written feature articles for local arts journals *Muse and Artlook*, had short stories published in *The Canberra Times, Royal Melbourne Institute of Technology Time To Write Anthologies*, and was shortlisted for The Fish Flash Fiction Award. He lives in Canberra, Australia with his partner, muse and soulmate, Stephanie.
E: jsstockdill@homemail.com.au

Jo Wilson-Ridley
Jo is a poet based in Queanbeyan, Australia. She has been published in *five bells, fourW, Feast of Poetry*, and on a postcard with the Ekphrasis Poetry Competition. After eleven years of living in the Riverina, Jo has spent the last year stalking politicians and slamming poetry in our country's Bush Capital. Jo has been a State Finalist in the Australian Poetry Slam in 2011, 2012, 2013 and in 2015 but is still picking up the best poetry lines from cheering on her sons at Junior AFL.
E: jo_wilson_ridley@hotmail.com

Justin Fox
Justin is a writer and photographer based in Cape Town, South Africa. He's a former editor of *Getaway International* travel magazine. Justin was a Rhodes Scholar and received a doctorate in English from Oxford University after which he became a research fellow at the University of Cape Town, where he now teaches part-time. His articles and photographs have appeared internationally in a number of publications and on a wide range of topics, while his short stories and poems have appeared in various anthologies. His recent books include *The Marginal Safari* (Umuzi, 2010), *Whoever Fears the Sea* (Umuzi, 2014) and *The Impossible Five* (Tafelberg, 2015).
E: justinfoxafrica@gmail.com

Karin Slater
"I am a Scottish poet and short fiction writer from the Outer Hebrides whose work has appeared in a number of publications. I graduated in Creative Writing from the University of Glamorgan back in 2006 and

have a keenness for poetry."
E: karin_2930@yahoo.com
Blog: Wordpress.karinslater.com

Karishma Krishna Kumar
Karishma is a freelance writer from India and has completed a Bachelor of Arts degree in English Literature from the University of Pune. As an avid traveller, she draws inspiration from the lives of people she's met during her explorations of the underbelly of her country. Her short stories and poetry feature on her website and blog. Raised in the Kingdom of Saudi Arabia and an introvert during her childhood years, she has also completed a Bachelor of Science degree in Visual Communication in Bahrain and finished her MBA in Public Relations from Symbiosis International University.
W: www.karishmakrishnakumar.com
Blog: www.morning-fire.blogspot.com

Kariuki wa Nyamu
Kariuki wa Nyamu is a highly artistic Kenyan poet, radio playwright, editor and high school teacher. He holds a BA in English, Literature and Education from Makerere University, Uganda. He started crafting excellent poetic pieces during his high school days. He has won Creative Writing competitions at school, university and national level. Apart from poetry and radio plays, he also writes film scripts, short stories, satirical essays as well as Children's tales. He is also an accomplished verse and public speaking coach, film enthusiast and music lover. His poetry appears in *A Thousand Voices Rising* (2014), *Boda Boda Anthem and Other Poems* (2015), *Best New African Poets 2015 Anthology*, *The Reeest Verses Poetry Anthology* (2016), *Jalada Africa 04: The Language Issue, Bonus Edition* (2016), *Parousia: A Christian Arts and Literary Magazine Issue II* (2016), *Dwartonline Literary Magazine Issue II* (2016), and also forthcoming in *Multi-verse: Kenyan Poetry in English Since 2003, Experimental Writing: Volume 1, Africa Vs Latin America Anthology, Babishai Niwe Children's Poetry Anthology*, among others. He is presently pursuing an MA (Literature) at Kenyatta University, Kenya. Poetry is certainly his territory.
E: nyamukariuki@gmail.com

Kathleen Bleakley
Descended from lighthouse keepers, Kathleen lives in Wollongong, Australia, between the sea and the escarpment. *Lightseekers* is her third book and second major collaboration with photographer 'pling. Kathleen and 'pling's previous publication is *Jumping Out Of Cars* with Andrea Gawthorne, 2004.

E: kathleen@pling.id.au
W: Inninderrapress.org.au/poetry

Kathleen Boyle
Kathleen Boyle *nee* Dodd, was born in Liverpool, where she spent her childhood years before leaving to train as a teacher in Hull in 1972. Kathleen has worked as a teacher in Hull, Leeds and Carlisle and international schools in Columbia, Bahrain and Cairo. She has written stories and poems throughout her life, publishing a collection of poems about growing up in 1950s Liverpool entitled, *Sugar Butties and Mersey Memoirs* as well as a collection of poems for children about a teddy bear called *Harry Pennington*. During her time in Bahrain she wrote *The Pearl House* a short story which spans the cultural divides of Liverpool and Bahrain. The story, together with her poems, *Bahrain* and *Umm Al Hassam* were published in the collections, *My Beautiful Bahrain* and *More of My Beautiful Bahrain*. Kathleen has written a series of childrens' stories for Beirut publishers Dar El Fikr, two of which, *The Jewel of the Deep* and *The Magic Pearl and Dilmun*, have now been illustrated and published. She has also contributed to *LONELY – A collection of poetry and prose about lonliness and being alone*, has written a novella; *Catherine of Liverpool*, and is presently working on the sequel. Now into her fortieth year as a teacher, she combines her love of travel with teaching and is presently based in Cairo, Egypt.
E: kathdodd@aol.com

Kathleen Coyle
Kathleen is a Scottish writer currently based in Glasgow. Since graduating from University of Strathclyde, she has had two short stories published. She also writes features for Glasgow based zine *TYCI*.
E: katdubs261@gmail.com
T: Twitter.com/coyle_kat

Kathleen Vallance
Kathleen lives in a rural Victorian town in the Wimmera region of North West Victoria, Australia. She works as a Learning Support Officer, and is a performing bush poet, both of the comedy and traditional Australian genre. She has won several performance competitions and has spent the last several years honing her stage and performance techniques. "Nothing thrills me like getting the spoken word out to audiences."
E: rkvall51@tpg.com.au

Katie Lewington
Katie is a widely published poet from the UK and likes to review the books she reads, listen to music, daydream, watch Cary Grant films, help *The Pithead Chapel* journal and *Transcending Shadows* review and *Punks Write Poems Press* sift through their submissions, sniff 50 year old poetry tomes and enjoy the aesthetic display of many literary magazines (she has been published in some of these) She has self published a collection of her own poetry and is currently focusing on finding a publisher for her (many) chapbooks. She reads widely and continues to help promote independent authors through social media.
E: katielewington@yahoo.com
Blog: Katiecreativewriterblog.wordpress.com
Twitter: @idontwearahat

Keith Nunes
Keith is from Lake Rotoma, New Zealand. He was a newspaper sub-editor for 20-plus years but after a nervous breakdown he moved into rural squalor and writes for the sheer joy of it. He's been published around NZ and increasingly in the UK and US. He is a *Pushcart Prize* nominee and his chapbook *Crashing the Calliope* is sold by the lunatic fringe. Keith has also contributed to *LONELY A Collection of Poetry and Prose on Loneliness and Being Alone*.
E: kwn@ihug.co.nz

Kev Milsom
Kev is in the early stages of his fifth decade and originates from Bristol, in the west of England. He currently writes for several magazines and websites, along with working for a small publishing company; focusing specifically on encouraging new writers. Here, he conducts interviews and reviews literature, particularly when it involves someone's first novel, or poetry. While he has had poetry and short stories published in several anthologies, Kev is still battling fiercely against the dreaded obstacle of 'completing a first novel'. Now, suitably armed with stronger anti-procrastination tools, he hopes to have something finished in 2017... possibly 2018 at the very latest.
E: kevmilsom@yahoo.co.uk

Kimmy Alan
Kimmy is a wannabe poet from the land of Lake Woebegone. A retired steel worker who was diagnosed with stage 4 cancer, Kimmy Alan pursed his love of poetry as a distraction while undergoing chemo and radiation. For him, poetry has proven to be a powerful catharsis as he is currently in remission. When he isn't writing he

spends time with his four wonderful nieces, whom he says: "are driving him to pieces."
E: kimmyalan@outlook.com

Kirsty A. Niven
Kirsty lives in Dundee, Scotland with her husband and cat. She graduated from the University of Dundee with a first class English degree. She was a featured poet on *Creekwalker* and her work has appeared in *Artificial Womb* and on *Mothers Always Write*. One of her poems is also currently on the Scottish Book Trust's website as part of their *Secrets & Confessions* project. Her poetry is due to appear in *The Dawntreader, Sarasvati* and the anthology *I Only Wanted One Time To See You Laughing*, as well as appearing for a second time on *Mothers Always Write* in the near future.
E: kaniven13@outlook.com

Lonita Nugrahayu
Born and growing up in Jakarta, Indonesia, Lonita is a home-maker now residing in the Kingdom of Bahrain. She finds writing therapeutic, and has been writing poetry on and off since childhood. At the moment she is focusing on polishing her work, but one day wishes to have her work published, as well as introducing poetry to younger generation as part of encouraging them to have more respect for the literary world. She also hopes to inspire and encourage other women to take up the pen and shape words into poems. She believes the best words are those that come from the heart.
E: lonitaan@outlook.com

Leon Stelmach
A late comer to creative writing and poetry having, for too long, been involved with the penning of business reports and plans. Now supported and inspired by friends and colleagues at Huntly Writers and, with a little more time to think, Leon is beginning to learn the writers trade. Still seeking metier, he is busy experimenting with everything from the Haiku to a short novel.
E: leon.stelmach@btopenworld.com

Lucy Reid
Lucy found writing at 14, when her first real story was read aloud. A stuffed full car ride several years later, would take her to the literary heart of Edinburgh. There her calling to write grew. Here she found herself in poetry, even performed her first reading. Dipped into her first ever screenplay. Dived into her first-love – prose. Now she spends her time searching the city for stories, and carries a little teal

notepad wherever she goes. Lucy has also contributed to *LONELY - A Collection of Poetry and Prose on Loneliness and Being Alone.*
E: lucyalannareid@gmail.com
Blog: Theimperfectreader.wordpress.com

Mandy Mullen
"I am a novice writer, not having written for over 37 years - heading for "The Big Hawaii 5.0." at the end of the year. First piece of writing was when I was 10 years of age where I wrote a poem about my dog Major for the school magazine - still think about him ! My teacher at the time used to read my stories out for Friday afternoon's entertainment! My first year teacher at secondary school entered a story I wrote into a library competition where I won a prize and had my picture in the local paper. My passion for writing has re-ignited with zest and I find I can't stop and started going to a Creative Writing club at my local library around six months ago. I hope now to pursue a career in writing. This (*LOVE*) is only the second entry of my work through, The Scottish Book Trust - the first being for *Secrets and Confessions*. My next contribution will be for The New Writer's Awards. I have decided to write under the name Mandy as my mum wanted to call me this when I was born but my dad thought Mandy Mullen' sounded daft!"
E: fatmammy@outlook.com

Madhumitha Murali
Madhumitha Murali is a fiction writer, poet and an MBA graduate. She is from Bangalore, India. She has published few poems with Seventh Quarry Magazine and has contributed to The Voices Project. She is currently looking for a publisher for her short story collections and poetry book. She is also working on a full length novel.
E: madhusana14@yahoo.com
Blog: Dailywritesmag.blogspot.in
Blog: Loveyourlifeinspiredbyself.blogspot.in

Marc Brightside
Marc is of Scottish/English descent, residing in his home-town of Croydon, South London. As a writer he specialises in contemporary, literary fiction for adults, and is currently working on his debut novel. Over the past few years he has contributed to *Vortex*, conducted workshops and poetry readings at the University of Winchester, and has worked as an editor of poetry and non-fiction for *Litmus 2016*, where his own work was described as displaying a sense of, "Occasionally shocking realism." Marc posts informally on his WordPress blog, *Rarely a Brighter Side*, and can also be found on Facebook and Twitter.

E: marcbrightside@yahoo.co.uk
Blog: Marcbrightside.wordpress.com
Facebook: Facebook.com/MarcBrightside
Twitter: Twitter.com/MarcBrightside

Martin Redfern
Martin lives in Edinburgh, Scotland. A publisher by occupation, he also writes short stories and poetry. Martin's recent work has appeared in a number of literary magazines including *The Puffin Review, Ink, Sweat and Tears, Far Off Places, Southlight* and *Obsessed with Pipework*. Martin was a runner-up in The Puffin Review's short story competition on the theme of Obsession.
E: mcr3@btinternet.com

Maxine Rose Munro
Maxine grew up in the Shetland Islands. Having never once set foot off the islands she left for Glasgow at age 18 and the subsequent culture shock has never left her. She still feels as if she is an islander, though one now adrift. Her poetry has appeared in *Northwords Now, The New Shetlander, Obsessed With Pipework* and *Artificium*, among others.
E: maxinerosemunro@gmx.co.uk

Megan Costigan
Megan Costigan is a public servant working in aged care policy and part-time writer. In addition to a range of poetry published in university literary magazine *Harvester USQ* (1989-1992) and several gay and lesbian magazines, she has had a short story published in (1997) *Pressing the Flesh - An anthology of emerging writers in the ACT* and a poem published in (2002) *Sappho's Dreams and Delights - An Australian Anthology of Lesbian poetry*. She is currently working on her first full-length novel.
E: blue4wren@bigpond.com

Megan MacLeod
"I am Megan MacLeod, novice poet, rambler of ideas and scribbler of thoughts. My private writing comprises of poems (or musings and rambling with ink to parchment). On a professional note, since 2002, I have written news releases, content for websites, client profiles, edited articles and features, and created tag-lines and body copy for advertising."
E: macleodmegan@hotmail.com

Michelle Lee
"I'm an associate professor of literature, fiction writing, and

composition at Daytona State College on the coast of Florida. For the past three years, I've also served as one of the poetry editors for *Rivet: The Journal of Writing That Risks,* based in San Francisco. I've published across genres, was invited to read my work at the University College London, and bear the Pushcart Prize nominee badge for my poetry. This past Spring, my work was published in the anthology, *All We Can Hold,* by Sage Hill Press. You can also find some of my recent fiction and poetry online at *Animal* Literary Magazine, *The Vignette Review*, and *The Citron Review*."
E: michelle.lee@daytonastate.edu

Molly Donald
"My name is Molly Donald from Glasgow, Scotland. I have been writing since I was welcomed into the world of doubl-digit ages. From writing on Wattpad, to writing with others in groups, and exploring the world of writing as much as my young brain can. I am soon to be attending City of Glasgow College, where I will be studying Creative Writing for a year before moving onto Uni to expand my knowledge of the writing world further. My career aspirations has always been to write, and write, and write more. There's nothing else in the world I want to do. I write about everything: the people I love, the strangers I meet, the things I feel."
E: yllomdonald@gmail.com
Tumblr: Writing-woes.tumblr.com

Nikita Krishna Kumar
"I am a 23 year old young woman with dreams and ambitions. I love, love; The concept, the feeling and all the emotions. I fell in love with the idea of being able to love unconditionally. This happened when I turned 20. I have been writing for as long as I can remember. I always felt better after writing thoughts and emotions. Facing an emotion was the one thing I was incapable of. Overtime I wrote about a variety of things. Love being one of them. My soul aim in life is to let everyone know how very beautiful they are. 'Love may seem like the most difficult thing a person does. Know that *Loving* is the easiest thing one does in a day'"
E: naina.k812@gmail.com

Nilanjana Bose
Nilanjana is a parent, writer, poet, blogger and a market research professional. Born in Kolkata, India, brought up in New Delhi and West Africa, her mailing address has changed some 15 times so far and she is always ready for the next change. She believes in travelling light, and a sense of humour, along with the passport, is top on her packing list. Dipping into other cultures and countries,

whether as an expat resident or a tourist, refreshes her writing muscles. She speaks English, Bengali and Hindi; and understands more Arabic than she can account for. She has a first class degree in Maths from Delhi University, a diploma in Marketing from Chartered Institute of Marketing, UK; and has lived/worked in India, Nigeria, Bahrain, UAE and Egypt. She celebrates the diverse range of cultural environments that she has experienced and her ability to navigate different landscapes of language, beliefs and customs. She has written over 2000 poems, 100s of short stories, flash fiction and essays, her writing is informed by her travels as well as her own heritage. Her poems, short stories, essays and travel memoirs have been published in both print and on-line. Her first book was a collection of short fiction in Bengali called *Seemaheen Bidesh (Foreign without Borders)*. Her work has appeared in print in *Ananda Lipi* (US), *Sabaya* (Bahrain), in multi-author anthologies like *Social Potpourri – An Anthology* and *10 Love Stories* released by Indiblogger and Harper Collins India in 2015, as well as online in e-zines like *eFiction India*. She was a contributing editor in *Inner Child* magazine (US) with her own byline *Passport to Our World* a travel feature which ran to a 24 part series., and contributed to *LONELY - A Collection of Poetry and Prose on Loneliness and Being Alone*.
E: nilabose306b@gmail.com
Blog: Madly-in-Verse

Norbert Gora
Norbert is a 26-years old poet and writer from Poland. He lives in a little town of Góra. Many of his horror, SF and romance short stories have been published in his home country. He is also author of many poems in English language poetry anthologies around the world.
E: norbert.gora@aol.co.uk

Pab Roberts
Pab is based in Scotland and writes on the themes of humour, magic realism, nature and loss. He was selected by Edinburgh UNESCO City of Literature Trust as Story Shop writer for the Edinburgh International Book Festival 2015. Previously publications include: *The Guardian, Leither Magazine, Freak Circus, The Pygmy Giant* and *Erica*.
E: pab_roberts@hotmail.com

Pallang Mofokeng
In South Africa, in the Eastern Cape, there lies a small city named Sterkspruit. There in Sterkspruit there's a small, tiny village of Walaza. The 1995 August on the 3rd, a son was born to the Bafokeng family by the name Pallang Mofokeng. He was born a first child to

Bukelwa Mpalweni who married to a family of the Sothos to Tukelo Mofokeng. Pallang is a young ambitious writer not yet with a name but his goal is beyond his writing.
E: Pallang639@gmail.com

Pamela Scott
Pamela is thirty five years old and lives in Glasgow, UK with her partner. Her poems and stories have been published in various magazines including *The New Writer, Carillon* and *Words with Jam*. Her poems have been published in anthologies by Indigo Dreams Press including *Crab Lines off the Pier*. Her poems and stories have won 2nd and 3rd place in various competitions including the Newark Poetry Society Competition and the Global Short Story Competition. She has completed two novels and is seeking publication / representation, and is working on a third novel and a series of short stories inspired by the seven deadly sins.
E: pamelascottwriter@gmail.com
W: Pamelascottwriter.com
Blog: Pscottwritingnotebook.wordpress.com
Blog: Thebookloversboudoir.wordpress.com
FB: Facebook.com/pamelascottwriter
Twitter: Twitter.com/pscottwriter

Rachel Walker
Rachel recently graduated from the University of Glasgow with a first class honours degree in English Literature and History. She currently writes short stories, features, and film and theatre reviews for various student magazines; acts as the Membership Engagement Officer for the Scottish Writers' Centre and is the present Creative Writing Editor of *qmunicate* magazine.
E: rlwalker1@hotmail.co.uk
Blog: Whatracheldidblog.wordpress.com

Rhyl Graham
Rhyl lives in Townsville NQ Australia. She has been writing poetry for many years but really fell in love with Australian Bush Poetry in 2007. She is a member of Townsville Bush Poetry Mates and loves to write of life's experiences.
E: rhyl_graham@aapt.net.au

Ronald L Kundinger
Ronald is a poet, painter, lamp builder and by trade an electrician. He has been writing poetry since he was a young lad and published quite a few poems in small press magazines in the late '90s and early 2000s.

E: ronksenior@yahoo.com

Rosie Mapplebeck
Rosie's stories and poems are from her deep experience of living among animals and birds and of magic. She loves sharing traditional tales, her stories and poetry to audiences where families and friends share together. She hosts live literary events in Ayr and takes story walks round Ayrshire. She co-owns a boarding cattery, offering holistic and healing care for animals. She studied botany with David Bellamy, has been a Special Constable, Veterinary Nurse and once ran a heavy metal disco. She is part of the Living Voices project which shares story, song and poetry with elders and those with dementia. She is presently creating a heritage trail for Ayr. You may also find her wild dancing; foraging plants for gastronomic delectation or caring for her bees. Rosie's poetry has been published by Glasgow Review of Books, Fairacre Press and Rosie has also contributed to *LONELY – A Collection of Poetry and Prose on Loneliness and Being Alone.*
E: rosiestories@ymail.com
W: www.rosiestories.com
FB: Facebook.com/rosie.mapplebeck

Ryan Joel
Ryan is 39 and as well as being an artist, he has a profound love affair with writing and literature in general. He has recently contributed *LONELY – A Collection of Poetry and Prose on Loneliness and Being Alone* and his love for prose and short musings are deep and thought provoking. He is passionate about pushing the boundaries of imagination and toying with the human condition. You have been warned.
E: rjoel@mweb.co.za
Twitter: @Captainrawrsome

Sara Spivey
Originally from London, Sara spent a number of years working in advertising, marketing and training in the West End before moving to Hong Kong as Associate VP for ESPN TV. She fell in love with the Far East and its emerging artwork scene, so when she relocated to Phoenix, Arizona in 2000, the US restrictions whilst waiting for her green card, propelled her to start her own business. This she did, becoming an independent art dealer specialising in Vietnamese paintings and Chinese sculpture, which was well received by the US and European markets. After spending 10 years in America she returned to the UK for a short period before moving to Egypt three years ago working as a teacher in Cairo. She comes from a small

family of journalists and published authors, publishing her own first novel in 2012 called *The Dragon of Hidden Treasures* aimed at the pre-teen market. Prior to this she had always focused on short story writing which she still loves creating. She currently has her second book *The Starbucks Soap* sketched out, and has recently contributed to *LONELY – A Collection of Poetry and Prose on Loneliness and Being Alone.*
E: sara_sparky@email.com

S'busiso Manqa
S'busiso is a South African born Poet, author and film-maker, who has recently published a book titled: *Understanding Life Through Poetry* (2016) and is currently a creative director in a media company based in South Africa called Octopus Vision. He has also collaborated in humanitarian projects with the International Association of Scientologists to inspire change in the townships of South Africa.
E: sbusisomanqa@gmail.com

Steve Howrie
Steve was born in Leicester, England, but lived in Scotland for more than twenty years, where he was a member of Bute Writers Group. Whilst on Bute, he developed his writing skills, won prizes for his short stories, and wrote two plays - one of which was staged in Scotland. For the past eight years, he has been living and working in China where he was an active member of the Suzhou Writers and Artists Group and self-published four books. He is also a songwriter with a catalogue of over thirty songs. His dream is to earn his living as a writer… "Maybe one day," he says. In the meantime, his day job is teaching Chinese high school students mathematics at an international school in Suzhou. He loves this part of China and finds it very inspirational.
E: steve.howrie@outlook.com
W: Smashwords.com/profile/view/spender

Trudy Duffy – Wigman
"I was born and bred in the Netherlands when nobody had stepped on the Moon yet and a telephone was a big Bakelite object. I graduated in Tourism, did a Master's Degree in Online Learning and taught Tourism in college. Now living in Scotland, I own and run a shop and try to write in the time left after selling buttons and ribbons. Two of my stories have been published in anthologies. I hope I can get a few more published. English is not my first language but it has become the language of choice when writing."
E: duffy.wigman@btinternet.com

Vaijayantee Bhattacharya
Vaijayantee is an editor and writer with over 12 years of editorial experience in the print and publishing media. She is currently associated as Editor of a few well-known magazines and publications. A poet at leisure, several poems of hers have been published in various publications including *LONELY - A Collection of Poetry and Prose on Loneliness and Being Alone,* and she is currently working at her own anthology of poems.
E: vaijayantee@gmail.com
W: Teatalkwithvaijayantee.weebly.com

Zahra Zuhair
"My first poem came to me when I was 14 years old. Since then, I have found much inspiration in the works of great poets and writers, most specifically Shelley, Rilke and Toni Morrison. They have moved me, captured me and freed me. Ten years later, I can say I have written all sorts of things, some I no longer have and some I love dearly. However, all of what I have written, whether good or bad, carries so much meaning to me, and I only hope that one day my writing will be as meaningful to someone else." Zahra has contributed to *LONELY - A Collection of Poetry and Prose on Loneliness and Being Alone.*
E: zahrazuhair.91@gmail.com
Blog: Keeeptalking.wordpress.com

Zondrae King
Proud of her Italian heritage but fiercely Australian, Zondrae writes and performs poetry on a wide range of topics, from 'empty nest syndrome' to mining. Zondrae performed at the first Snowy Festival in 2009 and won the Snowy Cup, and has appeared at festivals from Mackay Qld to Cobargo NSW. She is a multi-award winner, NSW Written Champion ABPA 2007, Poet of the Mountain at Mt. Kembla 2008, and regularly comes in the top five in writing competitions. Her work has been included in every addition of the *The Bronze Swagman* anthology from 2007 through to 2015, excluding 2013, and has been widely published elsewhere, including Award Winning Australian Authors. She will turn 70 later in 2016 year. Whether she shares with you a laugh or a cry, she is simply delighted to be included. She has recently been forced to slowdown because of advancing Parkinson's
E: zondraeking@gmail.com
W: www. abpa.org.au

Are You A Writer And/Or Poet?

I am looking for contributions from writers and poets, any age and from anywhere in the world, who feel they might like to contribute (in English) to one or more of our unique collections of poetry and short prose on particular topics and themes. No word count for poetry, maximum 1500 words for short prose. You can write under your real name or a pseudonym.

Because of the number of different contributions and contributors in each book, there is no payment though I'm afraid. Nor can I send a complimentary copy out to everyone either; because of the number of different contributors and countries represented in each book, it would just be far too expensive and we just couldn't publish otherwise. However I will send all contributors a pdf copy if requested, and all our books will be available at very competitive prices from thirteen Amazon websites worldwide, as both a larger format (6 inch x 9 inch or 15.24 cm x 22.86 cm) paperback and Kindle.

If you are interested in seeing your work published, and your words read, please send your contribution/s with the name of the Collection in the subject line, along with a brief writers' biography (100 - 200 words plus any contact details you want publishing e.g. your website, email, blog etc. plus your nationality and the country where you are currently based) to me to:

E: Editor@collectionsofpoetryandprose.com

If you love writing, wherever you are in the world, whatever your experience of writing, please do contribute!

Our next collection: **TRAVEL - A Collection of Poetry and Prose on Travels and Travelling**

Followed by:
- HAPPY - A Collection of Poetry and Prose on Happiness and Being Happy
- WAR - A Collection of Poetry and Prose about both the Bravery and Horror of War

You can submit to multiple Collections, and up to six pieces per Collection too! Go to: www.CollectionsofPoetryandProse.com

LONELY - A Collection of Poetry and Prose on Loneliness and Being Alone

Featuring 118 contributions from 57 writers in 26 countries, with many of the contributions reflecting the diverse backgrounds and cultures of the writers, and all writing in their own unique style, LONELY - A Collection of Poetry and Prose on Loneliness and Being Alone, is an extraordinary, unique and eclectic mixture of both traditional and modern verse, and short prose, from writers around the world.

Focusing on just about every aspect of loneliness and being alone, and covering topics as diverse as old age, bereavement, abandonment, divorce, entrapment, unrequited love, depression, trauma, failure and addiction, as well as the more abstract and esoteric, LONELY has been acclaimed worldwide for its diversity and mix of writers and styles.

Paperback £9.99 (GBP). ISBN: 978-1523912780
Kindle £3.99 (GBP). ASIN: B01DQLHF70

www.CollectionsofPoetryandProse.com

Printed in Dunstable, United Kingdom